I Was AFRAID of That!

Displacing Fear At The Core of Your Life

Robert Alan Collins

I Was Afraid of That!

Copyright © 2020-2021 Rob Collins | Media Ministries

Published by: GraceBrooke Creative | Metanoia Publishing

Layout Design: Rob Collins

Printed by: The Book Patch

ISBN-10: 1637901860

ISBN-13: 9781637901861

Cover Design: Heath Honaker - Machine Communications

Cover Photo: Madison Collins

Formatting: Heath Honaker / Rob Collins

Editing: Becky Watson

Printed in the United States of America

References not listed: Google

Unless otherwise noted, Scripture quotations are from *The Holy Bible: New International Version*®. NIV®. Copyright © 1973, 1978, 1984 by International Bible Society. Used by permission of Zondervan Publishing House. All rights reserved.

What Others Are Saying...

In his book, I Was Afraid of That! my friend Rob Collins gets vulnerable and genuinely addresses the thing we struggle with the most when everything turns upside down. For every person that has ever experienced fear, the kind that paralyzes your dreams before you even act on them, this book is for you. In it you will be reminded that you have no control over what happens to you, but you do have control over how you live and how you respond to being afraid.

- Bishop Tony Miller
Pastor of the Gate Church
Founder of The Destiny Network
Oklahoma City, Oklahoma

Fear is the barrier to most of the successes of your life. If ever there is a book needed writing, this is the book. We live in a world torn in pieces. Race, politics and pandemics are only partial ingredients to the elixir that fear has spread to every corner of society. In this uncannily timed book: I Was Afraid of That! Author Rob Collins not only puts his finger on the issue, (those alone are self-evident), he brings the most important of all things– the answer! Enjoy the read, better still, enjoy your freedom from fear itself.

- Philip D. Cameron
Evangelist, Author and Singer
President and Founder of the Orphan's Hands
Montgomery, Alabama

Every sentence in this book is loaded with life changing wisdom! I encourage you to step into your BEST SEASON as you apply the TRUTHS that this great author, Rob Collins pours into your life in regard to overcoming unhealthy fears! Rob has opened the door wide for you to step into GREATNESS and leave behind fear! You will equip your LIFE to live at NEXT LEVEL LIVING with a new found joy, peace and fortitude! If you're ready to embrace this New Season of opportunity to displace unhealthy fears at the core of your life, then this is the book for you!

- **Dr. Coy Barker**
International Orator, Author and Pastor
Legacy Builders, Monroe, Georgia

Fear is something we all face, and we don't just face it once. We need help confronting its many forms in every season of our life. Pastor Rob Collins offers honesty, wisdom, and years of experience that will help you overcome fear and experience all God has for you.

- **Dr. Jay Pike**
Executive Teaching Pastor – The Gate Church
Kings Gate College – Oklahoma City, Oklahoma

In a world plagued by fear there's never been a better time for this book written by my friend, Rob Collins. *I Was Afraid of That!* is Biblically sound and practical in content for life application. Keys, brass tacks if you will, on overcoming fear!

- **Luke Wren**
Worship Arts Pastor – 7 Hills Church
Florence, Kentucky

DEDICATION

This book is for anyone who has ever been afraid– afraid to think it, do it, speak it or say it. It's for anyone who has ever feared the past, the present or the future. It is also for anyone who has ever feared being right, being wrong or being misunderstood. *I Was Afraid of That!* is for the one who is afraid to take a chance or who is afraid to step up, or maybe even step out. It's for someone whom fear has hindered, held back, or has caused to feel helpless or even hopeless. If you have ever feared people's opinions, feared rejection or feared not being good enough, not having enough, or missing it– this book is for you! And, if this book is for you, then it's time for you to displace fear at the core of your life so you can be set free, to live again!

CONTENTS

DEDICATION - VII

NOTE FROM THE AUTHOR - XIII

INTRODUCTION - XXI

SECTION I – FEAR UNMASKED

Chapter 1 – The Origin
- Where It All Began - 39
- Still the Same Today - 42
- God Had a Plan - 44
- The Savior Shows Up - 48
- The Illusion Exposed - 49

Chapter 2 – Fear Defined
- What is Fear - 51
- Mild Uneasiness to Reverential Respect - 52
- Fight, Flee or Face It - 55
- Don't Allow Fear to Hinder You - 61

Chapter 3 – The Cause & Effect
- What Will You Do - 63
- Mind Matters - 64
- Interconnections - 68

Chapter 4 – No More Intimidation
- Covered - 73
- Awe, Reverence, Dread and Terror - 78

SECTION II – COMMON FEARS

Chapter 5 – Fear of Rejection
You've Already Been Accepted - 93
The Realities of Rejection - 100

Chapter 6 – Fear of Failure
Failure is Not Final - 105

Chapter 7 – Fear of the Future
The Unknown is Not Unknown to God - 113
You Can Be Certain - 117

Chapter 8 – Fear of Not Being Good Enough
Self-Image, Strengths and Uniqueness - 121
Compared to Whom-Compared to What - 125

Chapter 9 – Fear of Not Having Enough
Shutdowns, Shortages and Stockpiles - 131
Is More Than Enough Really Enough - 134

Chapter 10 – Fear of Missing It
What Does Missing It Really Mean - 141
Can You Really Miss It - 146

Chapter 11 – Fear of the Unknown
Don't Let That Stop You - 149
Do It Anyway - 152

Chapter 12 – Fear of Others' Opinions
Judgement, Persuasion and Value - 155

Applause, Criticism and Confirmation - 160

SECTION III – ASSUMPTIONS AND ANTIDOTES

Chapter 13 – Illusions and Realities
Shadows, Senses and Sounds - 167
Illusions, Assumptions and Self-Doubt - 171

Chapter 14 – Fear vs. Faith
Fear and Faith Both Produce Results - 175
See, Say, Do, Think and Believe - 177
Fear and Faith Both Engage Belief - 182

Chapter 15 – Antidotes to Fear
Face It or Forfeit Freedom - 187
Fear What Matters - 189
Let's Start Here - 191

Conclusion – Displacing Fear at the Core of Your Life
Finding A New Found Freedom - 195
A Few More Thoughts and A Prayer - 200

Special Thanks - 206

Additional Resources - 207

Social Media Links - 208

About the Author - 209

Endnotes - 210

For God has not given us a spirit of fear, but of power and of love and of a sound mind.
— II Timothy 1:7

NOTE FROM THE AUTHOR

It's my desire that you are encouraged, enlightened and empowered by reading this book. *I Was Afraid of That!* is personal to me because I have let fear rob me and hinder me in so many different scenarios of my life. The cover is even a testament of what I deal with inwardly at times. Up until this point, I've never done a personal photo of me as an adult on the cover of any of my books. Of course, I had to deal with the fear of what others would think or say about my doing that. Nonetheless, the title of this book is very personal in nature. As you know, it says, "I" was afraid of that! Therefore, I wanted a personal photo on the cover, declaring just that: "I" was afraid of that. That's right, past tense. Now with all of that being said, I want you to know that if you have dealt with issues of fear that have hindered you in your life, this book is for you!

If you have ever allowed fear to dictate your choices and rob you of your peace, it's time for you to displace fear at the core of your life! If you have ever dealt with fear on any level, I wrote this book with you in mind. And that's because I am tired of seeing people, myself included, who allow fear to rob them of experiences that they will never get back. Therefore, that's what this book is about. It's about displacing fear at the core of your life. Fear has hindered so many individuals in so many ways, for way too long. I want to see you set free to live your best life now free from all debilitating fear. I also want you to know that I can personally relate because I too have allowed fear to hinder me. It has stifled me in areas of my life where I could have flourished in greater ways, that is, if I wouldn't have allowed fear to dictate my decisions. Fear has also robbed me of moments that could have been more fully enjoyed. To illustrate, here's a personal story that explains what I mean when it comes to fear taking a moment from your life that you can never get back.

I actually hadn't thought about this story in years, until now, and here it is: *He called mom and dad and asked if it was ok for me to go and they said sure. It was my grandpa and he would be taking me to Kings Island Amusement Park in Mason Ohio, just outside of Cincinnati. Now, my grandfather was a big kid at heart. He loved sports, hunting, fishing and things that went fast. As a side note, he bought me my first gun and took me to my first high school state basketball championship game. We were very close and we shared a lot of first time experiences* together. This experience would be different. We were going to Kings Island near Cincinnati to ride the "Beast", that's right, the "Beast!"

At the time it was the 'fastest', 'tallest', 'baddest', 'longest', wooden roller coaster in the world. It sprawled over thirty-five acres of wooden terrain. The Beast broke all records when it opened April 14, 1979 as the longest and fastest ride in the world. It spans seven thousand three hundred and fifty-nine feet of rails and wood. The Beast includes a ride time of more than four minutes; vertical drops one hundred thirty-five feet (at a forty-five-degree angle); a one hundred twenty-five feet long underground tunnel at the bottom of the one hundred and thirty-five-foot drop; eight back turns – some to forty-five degrees; a five hundred forty-five-degree helix tunnel and speeds up to sixty-five mph.

But, that's not what scared me, because I didn't know any of that while standing in line with my grandpa waiting to ride the Beast. What scared me were the creaks, the rattles, the chain clicking noises, and the people screaming in the distance who were on the ride itself. I hate to admit it, but I let fear get the best of me that day and I stepped out of the line to ride the coaster. There were so many people in line I couldn't get back through the crowd of people to exit the ride. My grandpa *actually had to lift me over the wooden rail to exit the line that day and worst of all, he had to ride the Beast alone. He had taken me to specifically ride this ride with him, and I couldn't do it. I allowed fear to conquer me and ultimately decide my fate of not riding the Beast with my grandfather that day in 1979.*

I had just turned eleven years old and my grandpa was fifty-one when he took me to Mason, Ohio to ride the Beast; he would turn fifty-two later that same year. Ironically enough, I'm fifty-two years old as I am writing this book, and I hadn't thought about this day in years. That is, until I stood to do his memorial service in 2014. It had been thirty-five years since that day at Kings Island in Mason Ohio, standing in line to ride the Beast. But, as I stood that evening preaching the eulogy of my grandfather, I was wishing with everything in me that I had ridden the Beast with him that day.

Nonetheless, I went back to Kings Island in 1991 and conquered my fear by riding the Beast with some friends. But, when I did my grandpa's funeral service nothing could erase the sting of the memory that was lost, all because of fear. You see, fear will make you miss out on so much, especially if you don't learn to face it and conquer it, before it conquers you. It will cause you to have regrets and remorse. Fear is a robber and a thief. It is a paralyzer and a preventer. That's why I am writing this book. I don't want to see you, or anyone else be robbed by fear any longer. I want to see fear displaced at the core of your life, so that you can say, "*I Was Afraid of That!*" That's right, past tense!

I want you to know, you can overcome fear! Your mind has the ability to minimize or maximize what you think, feel or experience. And, what you feel, think or experience is where fear has the opportunity to live or die. You see, courage is not the absence of fear, it's the presence of mind to act when you are afraid. In other words, you may have to do it, say it or try it, all while being afraid. You may not always have the power to control how you feel, but you can't allow fear to make the decision in regard to what you do or don't do either.

You have the power to resist fear by acting in spite of being afraid. Learn to do what's right and best, even if you have to do it afraid. I realize now, that if I could have learned to conquer what I was thinking and how I was feeling, I would have enjoyed so many more aspects of my life. I could have had so many more memorable experiences, if only I would have done it anyway, regardless of how I felt or what I was thinking at the time. If I would have acted in spite of my fear, I could have experienced so much more!

Nelson Mandala says: *"Courage is not the absence of fear, but the triumph over it. The brave man is not he who does not feel afraid, but he who conquers that fear anyway."* That's why I wrote this book; I want to see you develop the courage it takes to not only overcome fear, but have the courage to act in spite of your fear. However, I also believe that some of the greatest factors of fear are not always spiders or heights, but deal rather with opinions, perceptions and ideals. I believe the greatest fears one may experience could deal with the concern of what others think or what an unknown outcome may produce.

I believe that being afraid of what others may think or being afraid of what you could look like if you said or did a particular thing can create greater fears than being afraid of the dark or a thunderstorm. Things like insecurities, perceptions, opinions believed and lies spoken, can fuel the personal fears like none other. For example, I know first-hand how religion, people's opinions, and personal insecurities can produce unhealthy fears in one's life that are everlasting and continually hindering. That's why I want you to know that embracing fear instead of resisting fear, will stifle, hinder, and limit every area of your life. Fear not dealt with will eventually affect everything you do and how you do it. This can include the simplest things or the most complex scenarios. Undealt with fear will keep you inhibited, causing you to not try something new or avoid things that have an unknown outcome.

Fear can cause you to forfeit so many memories. It can also cause you to flee or freeze, making you miss out on moments that although may have been frightening, would not have been harmful. While reading this book, I want you to rethink what you may be thinking and reevaluate what you may be placing too much value on. I want you to walk in a newfound freedom. I'm weary of seeing good people bound by their negative thoughts, familiar scenes and tainted perceptions! These scenarios produce fear, keeping you bound, not allowing you to experience true love, real peace and abundant joy! It's time for you to displace fear at the core of your life. It's time for you to be able to say, *I Was Afraid of That!* That's right, past tense. Now, let's get started!

INTRODUCTION

It's ironic, that as I write this book, the world is in the midst of a pandemic with the COVID-19 Novel Coronavirus. What an unusual moment of uncharted territory and uncertain times. What's even more ironic is that I've had this book idea and the title for about seven years and that I am just writing it, in the midst of this COVID-19 pandemic. I am now writing this introductory paragraph on the actual Monday after coming off of fourteen days of self-quarantines and social distancing. And, we just found out last night that, as a country, we are in for thirty more days of the same stipulations and protocol.

You talk about fear mixed with uncertainty. These are unparalleled and unprecedented times, to say the least. People are panicking. There have been weeks of bizarre binging and buying– especially the unusual purchasing of toilet paper. That's right, stores can't keep toilet paper on the shelves. Disney World and Disney Land have been shut down. The famous NCAA March Madness men's basketball tournament was cancelled. Opening day of major league baseball was cancelled. NASCAR racing has been suspended indefinitely. NBA basketball has been suspended indefinitely as well. Graduations and weddings have been postponed and/or cancelled for the time being. Restaurants have closed, schools and colleges have been dismissed, and beauty salons and barbershops have been closed until further notice. However, in all of these instances, I believe the worst case scenarios were in regards to family and friends not being able to attend the funerals of loved ones, and family members not being present for surgeries or visits to a family member or friend in the hospital.

Life as we know it, has been placed on hold. And, the uncertainty we are being faced with in this present day has produced a definite unsettledness for the future. This is producing an undercurrent of panic and fear around the globe. Nevertheless, I believe it is more of a fear of the unknown, than it is just a fear of the actual virus itself. Some have it and don't even realize it, while others have severe noticeable symptoms. There are numerous people who have mild cold or flu-like symptoms, while others have died from the same virus. It is mysterious and has been named a silent enemy.

People are being cautious, washing their hands, using hand sanitizer, wearing protective masks, and practicing social distancing and self-quarantining.

However, the greatest concern is the uncertainty and the unknown that we are faced with each day. When will this pandemic come to an end? How will it end? And when will we get back to a new normal? Will the economy recover? When will people go back to work? Will the school year resume this year or not? Will we ever have opening day of major league baseball? Will couples finally have their wedding day? And, will the graduation ceremonies take place for this year's graduates? Will there be food, water and toilet paper in the stores again? When will we go on vacation, shop at a mall or return to church? These questions present the unknown while producing uncertainties for everyone all around the globe.

I couldn't help by starting off talking about the COVID 19 pandemic because, in reality, it has affected the entire world and it is on the forefront of everyone's mind right now, including mine. And, it is producing so much unsettledness, uncertainty and, you guessed it: *Fear*! Fear is infiltrating people's lives and dominating their conversations. However, I want you to know that although many people are fearful and doubtful, many people are stepping up and helping in so many ways as well. People are helping others who can't help themselves by getting groceries, prescriptions and personal items. Many are bombarding social media to help encourage others through a song, a message or a meme. Others are picking up the phone and calling people to check on them to make sure they are o.k. It's amazing to see that people of faith and the church rising to the occasion. It is also amazing to see what can happen when we push back our fears and focus on what truly matters!

Coronavirus is a real thing. But, is the fear and panic surrounding it a proportionate response to this unknown virus causing a pandemic? Viruses, sickness and death are realties. However, fear is also a virus, highly contagious and can be equally as damaging. Fear is a destroyer, not a creator, fed by the overwhelming sense of the unknown. How many ventures, lives, economies, and ideas in human history were lost, damaged, left unaccomplished, or even not begun at all, because people were afraid of something? I don't want that to be your reality any longer! It's not healthy for you to live in fear. It is not beneficial for you either, especially if fear hinders you from prospering in any area of your life. You can conquer and triumph over any unhealthy fear that hinders you in your life! Troubles and trials will pass, provided you don't set up camp and stay in the middle of them. And, whether it's the Coronavirus or your own personal endeavors, do what you can do, have faith, believe God, and keep moving. Don't let fear stop you from becoming all that you can be!

This book however, is NOT about the COVID-19 (Novel Coronavirus) or the pandemic it has caused. It is about displacing fear at the core of your life so that you can say with me: "*I Was, Afraid of That!*" The title of this book is obviously, a play on words. I love *plays on words* and I have had this title and these thoughts in my heart and head for a while now. Let me explain the title. It's a double-entendre that could mean: "*I was afraid that might happen*", or "*I used to be afraid of that, but I am not afraid anymore!*" When you are finished reading this book, I want you to be able to say *I Was Afraid That!* which means, fear no longer operates at the core of your life! And, if you don't get anything else, I want you to get this: *"Most fears are usually bigger in your heart and head than they are in reality."*

Fear presents itself in so many forms and it shows up in so many different areas of our lives. It can show up in such a camouflaged manner, that it's not recognized as the enabler that it is. Fear presents itself in so many various ways and on so many different levels.

Sometimes we don't even recognize that it is actually fear that is the root of so many of the issues and problems that we are experiencing in our daily lives. Fear is a robber. Fear is a thief. It will rob you of your joy and steal your peace. That is, if you let it. That's the key! You can't let it! You can't allow it to take root or it will grow and entangle every area of your life imaginable. Fear will make you irritable and irrational. Fear will cause you to freeze when you should be moving. Fear will cause you to stop when you should keep going. It will stop you from doing what you know you should do. It will hinder you from doing what you know you can do. Fear is a double-edged sword that will destroy you when it is left unchallenged.

Here's what I mean by a double-edged sword. Fear can do one of two things. It can keep you from touching a fire or jumping off of a steep embankment. Which, by the way, is healthy! But, fear can also keep you from speaking up when you know you're right or keep you home when you need to get out and get something done. That is NOT healthy. Fear is based upon experience, knowledge and belief. It is also based upon feelings, perceptions, sight, and senses. Therefore, any or all of these indicators could determine how you experience or encounter fear. The double-edged sword scenario reveals that there is a healthy fear and an unhealthy fear. There is a fear that protects and guides and there is a fear that restricts and inhibits. Don't allow an unhealthy fear to cause you to develop unhealthy thoughts, patterns, or responses! Unhealthy fears are unhealthy and healthy fears are healthy and how you define the difference will determine what you experience in life.

For some, fear is fantastic and a friend. While for others of us, fear is horrible and a burden. No matter what the case may be, there is a healthy fear and an unhealthy fear. Fear is experienced through our senses and surroundings. However, most would also agree that fear is not only a feeling, but is also an *emotion* that determines and dictates various reactions and expressions. This emotion is induced by a perceived danger or threat, causing physiological behaviors and ultimately behavioral changes such as fleeing, hiding, screaming, crying and even freezing in place. Any or all of these behavioral changes can take place when the emotion of fear is experienced or a danger or threat is perceived or encountered.

Fear is defined in the dictionary as *"an unpleasant emotion caused by the belief that someone or something is dangerous, likely to cause pain, or is a threat"*. The Bible primarily defines two different types of fear: One is *phobos, a fear that either keeps us bound up with terror or causes us to flee in face of the unknown.* As a side note, the Bible has hundreds of scriptures telling us not to have this kind of fear. The other word in the Bible for fear is *yirah*, which deals with *awe and respect.* This type of fear keeps us safe from consequences. It's a healthy fear. Now as you can see, fear can be developed in one's life, defined in a dictionary or it can be diagnosed by psychologists and physicians.

There are various diagnosed fears and phobias in the world, and we will look at some of these in this book as well. However, what I want to deal with primarily are the practical fears that hinder so many of us in our daily routines of life and in our interactions with others. These are fears such as being afraid of what others may think, the fear of not being good enough, the fear of being wrong, the fear of being misunderstood, the fear of the unknown, the fear of not having enough, or the fear that things will never change or be any different than they are right now at this very moment.

I want to see these types of fears abolished at the core of your life. I want to expose any unhealthy fear that tries to hinder you. I want you to be set free from a fear that inhibits and stifles. I want to see you set free from fear that tries to stop you. I want to see you set free from a fear that tries to keep you from your purpose or from reaching your full potential in life. I also want you to remind you again that there are healthy fears. These fears are learned as well though. They keep you safe, they create healthy boundaries and they can keep you from harm or alert you of danger.

Nonetheless, I'm not talking about that kind of fear when I talk about displacing fear at the core of your life. I'm talking about a fear that hinders, kills, and stifles normal activities. I'm talking about the kind of fear that endeavors to keep you from new experiences, experiences that would benefit you, help liberate you, and ultimately empower you as a human being. I want to expose the fears that are unhealthy and that hinder you from being all that God has created you to be. I want to help remove the illusion that living with that kind of fear is o.k. I want you to experience the reality of living in freedom, freedom from a fear that binds and hinders.

Fear is an illusion that can distort reality and keep you from knowing, seeing, or experiencing what's on the other side of the very thing you fear the most. There is peace and joy and hope on the other side of the fear that is trying to hold you back right now. I pray the scales fall off and I pray that your eyes, heart and mind are empowered, enlightened and opened. I want to see you on the other side of what you fear the most, realizing that there wasn't anything to fear to begin with. I want to see you liberated and set free! I want to hear you say *I Was Afraid of That!* That's right, past tense– I used to be, but I am no longer!

As I write this book today and look back over my life, I can see where fear has hindered me and held me back in so many different areas of my existence. In some ways it has been marginal, but in other ways it has been monumental. I have dealt with many types and levels of fears; some have been merely surface level fears, while others have been more in depth and deeply rooted type fears. It has ranged from the simplest things such as being afraid of the dark, or a thunderstorm at night as a kid, to as an adult being afraid of what others may think, or being afraid of trying something that is new or different. Here's the deal! No matter your age or level of maturity, fear is something that we all deal with at some point or the other in our lifetime.

Remember, we've already agreed that there are healthy fears that help us by creating restraints and boundaries. They create safety and protection for us many times in life. A healthy fear will cause you to prepare while an unhealthy fear will cause you to avoid what needs to be done. You also need to remember that there is the fear of *reverence* and *awe* that you should have for God, His Word and His Ways. And, as you probably already know, there are many thoughts, opinions and perspectives in respect to fear.

Nevertheless, regardless of what your opinion is about fear, my opinion is: I don't believe it was ever God's intent for His creation to live in fear, especially, a fear that torments or hinders. That kind of fear is NOT from God. It is my hope that through this book, the Holy Spirit will enlighten, equip and empower you to rise up in a newfound courage to face those unhealthy fears, in a healthy manner. Not dealing with those unhealthy fears will create limitations that will ultimately hinder you from a life of freedom and peace.

I don't believe fear was ever God's intention and, for that matter, it was never mentioned until the fall of humankind; therefore, it is not only part of the creation account, but, it is also part of the curse. Adam and Eve sinned through disobedience in the Garden of Eden. However, Jesus became the second Adam and restored what was lost through obedience to God in the Garden of Gethsemane. Jesus came so that your joy may be complete and so that you may have peace. When fear is displaced at the core of your life, your joy will become full and your peace will become a reality.

The word *fear* was mentioned for the first time ever in the creation account in the book of Genesis in the Bible. As I said earlier, it is where Adam and Eve had sinned through disobedience. It Is it recorded like this in Genesis 3:6-11: *⁶When the woman saw that the fruit of the tree was good for food and pleasing to the eye, and also desirable for gaining wisdom, she took some and ate it. She also gave some to her husband, who was with her, and he ate it. ⁷Then the eyes of both of them were opened, and they realized they were naked; so they sewed fig leaves together and made coverings for themselves. ⁸Then the man and his wife heard the sound of the Lord God as he was walking in the garden in the cool of the day, and they hid from the Lord God among the trees of the garden. ⁹But the Lord God called to the man, "Where are you?" ¹⁰He answered, "I heard you in the garden, and I was **afraid** because I was naked; so I hid." ¹¹And he said, "Who told you that you were naked? Have you eaten from the tree that I commanded you not to eat from?"*

First of all, it's interesting that fear was one of the first emotions that was expressed and experienced by the new and first creation of humankind, Adam and Eve. It is also interesting to me that it was when they *heard the sound* of the Lord walking in the garden that they hid themselves. Isn't it true that *sounds* still enhance or create fear? Regardless, when they experienced fear for the very first time, the very first thing they did was hide and cover themselves with fig leaves.

I mean, wow! Can't you relate? When you're afraid the first thing you do is hide and the second thing you do is try to cover yourself from what it is you fear. If you hide and cover yourself, there's a sense that what you fear won't see you and you won't see it. We do this physically, but we also do this emotionally, relationally and spiritually. We hide and we close ourselves off from what we fear. We build walls and excuses to hide behind so we don't feel vulnerable or threatened by anything or anyone that will be a threat or danger to us.

But, here's the good news, God sent Jesus to help you, love you and empower you. He came to set you free! And, whom the Son sets free is free indeed, and there is now no condemnation for those who are in Christ! I also want you to know that this book is not to condemn you for having feelings or emotions that produce fear. This book is to help you to be set free from any fear that keeps you bound, hindered, or limited in any way. *I Was Afraid of That!* deals with revealing what needs to be dealt with, so that you can be empowered to live the best life you can right now.

Don't hide behind what is hindering you from healing and wholeness. What you cover remains concealed, but what you uncover becomes revealed. And what's revealed can be healed! When you sense and know the love of God, you will uncover your guilt, your hurts, your shame, and yes, even those unhealthy fears that are hindering you. And, what you uncover can be healed and covered by God's love, mercy and grace, a love, mercy and grace that will empower you to live differently and to become more!

If you are in Christ, you have been given the power of love and a sound mind. A sound mind causes peace, and when you experience fear, your sound mind has the power to refocus and recalibrate, until it once again creates a peace that is desired. Your mind is the control center that has to be renewed through the Word of God, which is Truth, and it's the Truth that will set you free from a fear that is unhealthy and that continues to hinder you.

Adam and Eve had sinned through disobedience, so they were afraid and hid themselves. But, God kept his end of the deal, He showed up, even though they had been disobedient. You see, sin doesn't change God; it changes us. God said, *"Where are you?"* Adam said, *"I was afraid, so I hid."* God's position remained the same; Adam's position had changed. God desired a relationship. Adam desired isolation. Love desires relationship. Fear desires isolation. Fear entered in by one man, but Jesus became the second Adam and perfected love and that perfect love casts out all fear.

When we experience fear, the tendency is still to run and hide and take cover. However, just like in the story with Adam, God will always come to us, even in our fear. God doesn't leave us in our fear, to be isolated. He comes to us to empower us. He stood by Adam, Noah, Moses, Jeremiah, Gideon, Mary (the mother of Jesus), and Paul (who wrote over half of the new Testament). He stood by them when they were afraid, and He will stand by you when you are afraid as well! And, As He said to them, He is saying to you: *"Don't be afraid, take courage, for I am the Lord your God and I am with you!"*

Jesus is not an enabler, He is the One who empowers, and He is with you!

I Was Afraid of That! is all about helping you displace fear at the core of your life. It's about exposing those fears that hinder, stifle, and that endeavor to stop you from being everything God has intended for you to be. I believe that there is always a root that causes fear to be established in our lives. I also believe when this root is revealed, you can be healed and empowered to rise above it. Then you can walk right past what you feared, into a newfound freedom that will produce a greater peace, joy and contentment in your life. Let's get started with the book!

SECTION I
Fear Unmasked

Chapter 1

The Origin

WHERE IT ALL BEGAN

I don't know what that day would have been like, but it must have been horrible. Creation was hiding in guilt, shame, regret and *fear*, from its creator. Innocence had been lost and the pain and regret of disobedience was felt and experienced for the very first time. Until now, Adam had walked with God and had enjoyed life with no shame, no regret or no *fear*. God created Adam and walked with him in the cool of the day in perfect fellowship, untainted. Until this point, Adam was alone and not afraid. He tended to the land and had no fear. Adam named all the animals and never feared, *"Was that the right name for that creature?"* Or, *"I wonder what the Lord thought about the name for that one?"*

Fear has been around almost from the beginning. It became a reality when Adam confessed and expressed the emotion he was feeling from the disobedience that had just taken place. He said, "I was naked and *afraid*." Vulnerability is always linked with fear. In Genesis chapter three it tells us that when Adam and Eve ate

I Was AFRAID *of That!*

from the tree in disobedience, they hid themselves because they were naked and afraid. Fear had never been in the equation until sin had been given birth to and Adam and Eve experienced its consequences for the very first time in a moment of regret, confusion and sorrow. This was literally in the beginning of all things. And, the idea of being afraid was mentioned and recorded for the first time in Genesis, which is the book of beginnings.

It was in this creation narrative that we see the ideal of *fear* appear for the very first time. It is also where Adam first spoke about *being afraid* when he said, *"I heard Your voice in the garden and I was afraid because I was naked, so I hid myself."* Adam was the first living being of all creation, created in the image of God. Adam and Eve were experiencing *fear* because of their disobedience, which had stripped them of their innocence and caused them to experience for the first time ever, for anyone, anywhere, the sense of *being afraid*. Fear caused them to hide and camouflage themselves. However, it created a moment for God to respond and to uncover what had happened that originally caused the *fear* to begin.

Chapter 1: The Origin

Adam said, *"I heard Your voice in the garden and I was afraid because I was naked, so I hid myself."* And God said, *"Who told you that you were naked?"* Notice Adam expressed his heart and gave the reason for his fear. Nonetheless, God dealt with what had caused the fear, not the fear itself. He said, *"Who told you that you were naked?"* He didn't say, *"Don't be afraid!"* or, *"Why are you afraid?"* He didn't even say, *"Why did you hide?"* He said. *"Who told you that you were naked?"* In other words, when you get to the root of the cause or condition of the fear that you are experiencing, it's then that you can begin to deal with the fear itself.

How did Adam even know it was *fear* that they were experiencing? Could it have been that just like with the naming of the animals through the declaration of his spoken words, Adam had the authority, through his verbalized words to determine and declare how he was feeling as well? He named and expressed what he was feeling, through his confession to the Lord. Here's what he said: *"I was afraid, because I was naked."* In other words, Adam and Eve's condition produced the awareness of being afraid and his confession defined the experience with the word *fear* for the very first time. *"This is why we feel afraid."* And, even if we don't always confess it, we usually in some way express it.

STILL THE SAME TODAY

I fully understand that Adam was awakened to newfound senses and stripped of innocence. However, I also believe the serpent that was more cunning than any beast of the field overshadowed Adam and Eve with fear and intimidation while enticing them to doubt and disobey. Intimidation is usually felt when being faced with something that causes you to fear. He began with the fear of "missing out" by using the fear that God was somehow withholding information from them. Could Adam and Eve have feared not being included or informed because they doubted God's love? Could they have believed He was not being completely honest with them in His admonishment in regard to the trees in the garden and their eating of its fruit? No matter the case, their disobedience and belief in a lie, produced fear, shame, guilt, and unworthiness.

The enemy's tactics are still the same today. He will use intimidation, doubt and fear to discourage and deter you in ultimately trying to defeat you. Could it have been that his tactic was fear and intimidation, not just doubt? We know he used doubt when he said, *"Did God really say, don't eat of every tree in the Garden?* Nonetheless, another type of fear could have been activated by the doubt the serpent cast. Fear comes in

Chapter 1: The Origin

many shapes and sizes. Could they have been afraid of missing out? Could they have been afraid that God was withholding something from them? Maybe they feared God didn't love them because there was something He was trying to withhold from them?

I believe the plan is still the same today. The plan is to get you to doubt God's Word so that you will doubt God's love. This in turn will establish the fear of being rejected, and of not being accepted. It will create a mindset of not feeling loved, accepted or worthy of God's desire for relationship. The serpent's ultimate plan was to entice Adam and Eve by appealing to their sensual and selfish desires and then ultimately striving to defeat them through isolation, separation and the *fear* of not measuring up or being good enough.

Fear separates and isolates. Love liberates and embraces. I believe fear was the ultimate plan of the enemy. Satan wants to make us feel isolated and separated from God. Nonetheless, God's plan is to embrace us in our fear and empower us to be set free from fear. This story of Adam and Eve reveals the origin of fear, but it also reveals the origin of God's plan for redemption. In this original encounter with fear, God shows up to His creation that is being overwhelmed

with fear, and He will do the same for you. He will meet you where you are. That's the original plan: an untainted, unhindered relationship with God, your creator and redeemer.

The origin of something is important. An origin is where something begins; it is the place where it is established. The emotion of feeling afraid was experienced and originated by the first living creation of all creation, Adam. This chapter is about the origin of fear, it is about taking a look at where fear began and was established. In doing so, you will have a greater advantage in regards to displacing fear at the core of your life. Now, again, I know not all fear is bad or unhealthy. I also know not all fear is evil in origin either. However, I also believe there would have never been the emotion of fear being experienced in a negative, debilitating and crippling manner without sin being in the equation either.

GOD HAD A PLAN

With all of that being said, by one man, sin entered into the world, and by one man, sin was abolished. Adam was that man by whom sin entered the world and Jesus was that one man, by whom sin was abolished. Jesus became the second Adam and established for us

Chapter 1: The Origin

a new bloodline. Now, if sin was part of the original Adamic bloodline, then fear is part of the curse of sin. The good news is, Christ redeemed all that was lost through Adam and Eve's disobedience. Consequently, we have no reason to fear! The Bible tells us that perfect love casts out all fear. Jesus demonstrated God's love for mankind so that we can walk boldly and securely as the beloved of God without fear or reservation. Here are some scriptures to help establish what I've been saying:

I Corinthians 15:45-49

45And so it is written, "The first man Adam became a living being." The last Adam became a life-giving spirit. 46However, the spiritual is not first, but the natural, and afterward the spiritual. 47The first man was of the earth, made of dust; the second Man is the Lord from heaven. 48As was the man of dust, so also are those who are made of dust; and as is the heavenly Man, so also are those who are heavenly. 49And as we have borne the image of the man of dust, we shall also bear the image of the heavenly Man.

I John 4:17-18

17Love has been perfected among us in this: that we may have boldness in the Day of Judgment; because as He is, so are we in this world. 18There is no fear in love; but perfect love casts out fear.

John 3:16-17

16For God so loved the world that He gave His only begotten Son, that whoever believes in Him should not perish *but have everlasting life. **17**For God did not send His Son into the world to condemn the world, but that the world through Him might be saved.*

Isaiah 41:10

10*Fear not, for I am with you; be not dismayed, for I am your God. I will strengthen you, Yes, I will help you, I will uphold you with My righteous right hand.*

You can see from these scriptures what I've been talking about in regards to the origin of fear and how the second Adam, Jesus, restored all things through love and reconciled us to God through Himself. I also hope that you can see by now that I am establishing the fact that fear was something that originated in the very beginning of all creation, in the Garden of Eden.

The emotion of fear was experienced first by Adam the first creation of all mankind who was created in the image of God. And, these scriptures also show us how God's redemptive purpose was to bring us His love and to restore what had been lost and stolen through disobedience in the Garden of Eden. Jesus, in another garden, the Garden of Gethsemane, through surrender and obedience ended what began in one garden, the Garden of Eden, by Adam through selfishness and disobedience.

Chapter 1: The Origin

God had and has a plan for fear. As a matter of fact, every time fear is mentioned in the Word, or anytime someone experienced fear in the Bible God showed up. The Lord showed up in some form or the other and said, *"Fear not!" "Be of good cheer!" "Take courage!"* or *"Do not be afraid!"* He shows up to confront, comfort and admonish us in our fear. He desires to be with us; He longs to have an unhindered, untainted relationship with us, His creation.

In the book of Mathew where the Christmas story is recorded, it gives us a picture of God's plan when he reveals the ideals of redemption and relationship. In chapter one verse twenty-one, the writer says, *"His name will be called Jesus, for He shall save His people from their sin."* And in verse twenty-three of this same chapter Matthew tells us, *"And they shall call His name Emanuel, which is translated, God with us."* In this passage in the book of Matthew where Jesus (the second Adam) is being introduced, Matthew reveals redemption (v.21) and relationship (v.23). Redemption– *Jesus saves us from our sin.* Relationship– *God with us.* Ever since mankind fell in the Garden, God had a plan for redemption and relationship, for and with His creation. He came so that we would have no real reason to fear.

THE SAVIOR SHOWS UP

And, again, every time mankind experienced fear in the Bible, God showed up. He showed up to Adam, Noah, Gideon and Moses. He showed up to Mary the Mother of Jesus, Mary at the empty tomb, His disciples in the storm, and to Paul in transition, turbulence and trouble. He showed up on many occasions for various reasons. When He showed up it was always the same. His reason for saying, *"Don't be afraid"* always pointed to Him, His plan and to who He was. He is Faithful, Holy, Righteous and Just. He is longsuffering and an ever present help in the time of need. He will never leave you nor forsake you; He will be with you to the very end. The Lord establishes your steps and He sees your end from the beginning and your beginning from the end. He is the same yesterday, today and forevermore. He is faithful and most of all He is love! Therefore, there is no reason to fear.

That's the reason for my writing this book. I want to see you set free from any fear that keeps you from becoming all that you could become. I want to see you stop living in fear and regret. I want to see you freed from a fear that hinders and haunts you. Fear, by far, is the leading cause of regret! It is a destroyer, not a creator, fed by many things. How many ventures, lives, economies, and ideas in human history were lost, damaged, left unaccomplished, or even not begun at all, just because people were afraid of something? I don't want that to be the case for you anymore. I want to see you displace fear at the core of your life, especially an unhealthy fear that hinders you from being all that you were created to be!

THE ILLUSION EXPOSED

This chapter has been about the origin of fear- where it began, where it was established, and most importantly, through whom it can be broken and abolished. Could you imagine never being afraid? Can you imagine never experiencing the emotion of fear? Could you imagine literally walking with God in daily communion and conversation that was unhindered and uninhibited by anything or anyone? This is what Adam experienced. It would have been the purest form of innocence ever. But, through disobedience, Adam was robbed of that innocence and for the first time fear was experienced. That's the origin of fear. But, God doesn't leave us in our fear, He comes to us to intervene because He wants us to be comforted, helped and empowered. He didn't leave Adam alone in his fear, and He won't leave you alone in yours either!

I Was AFRAID of That!

Fear is an illusion that can distort reality and keep you from knowing, seeing, or experiencing what's on the other side of what you fear most. It's a smokescreen that will keep you from seeing things the way that they truly are. I don't want to see you or anyone else be so held by a fear that it keeps you from experiencing all that God has for you. I don't want you to be so gripped by fear that you never know the true joy of surrender or obedience. I don't want to see you stopped or hindered any longer. I don't want you to live another day with fear robbing you of your joy, hope or peace.

Fear is meant to keep you where you are. It will destroy relationships and stifle growth. Fear will keep you from moving forward and making progress. Nonetheless, Jesus came to empower and liberate. The Lord in His Word says over and over again, "Do not be afraid." Fear began in the garden but ended on the cross. It began with Adam and ended with Jesus. Love has been perfected through the person of Jesus Christ and perfect love casts out all fear. Don't allow what you fear the most, keep you from what you desire the most. It's time to displace fear at the core of your life!

Chapter 2

Fear Defined

WHAT IS FEAR

Fear is an illusion that can distort reality and keep you from knowing, seeing, or experiencing what's on the other side of what you fear most. Fear is an emotion that can be experienced in numerous ways and it causes a myriad of responses and reactions. It can be experienced from what is an actual reality, or it can be experienced from things that have been imagined and are not an actual reality at all. Fear can obscure reason and intensify emotions. It can cause one to freeze or flee. Fear can also be a concern, an apprehension, an anxiety or an agitation. Fear is an emotion that is experienced, felt or sensed by an individual when the possibility that something unpleasant or unwanted could occur.

Fear is a distressing emotion aroused by an impending danger, evil, pain, despair, etc. Regardless of whether the threat is real or imagined, the feeling or condition of being afraid is experienced. Fear is also something that can cause feelings of regret, dread or

apprehension. Fear can be an anxious concern caused by emotion, or it can be a profound reverence and awe towards God. Don't allow what you fear the most to keep you from what you desire the most. I want you to remember this throughout this book: "*Most fears are usually bigger in your heart and head than they are in reality.*" It's not that fear is not real; it's just that most of the things you experience that cause or create fear have a delusional factor that is hidden in a false reality.

MILD UNEASINESS TO REVERENTIAL RESPECT

So, what is fear? And, how do you define it? Well, let's start with the Bible. In the Bible, there are two basic and common words for *fear: yirah and phobos. Phobos*, is a fear that either keeps you bound up with terror or causes you to flee in face of the unknown. It's where we get our word for fear, *phobia. Phobia* is defined as *an exaggerated usually inexplicable and illogical fear of a particular object or situation*. *Phobos* is the word used in the Bible to describe an exaggerated fear. It's a fear that keeps you bound or that causes you to flee.

This kind of fear would be considered and defined as a fear that is unhealthy. This kind of fear will keep you bound, not allowing you to accomplish or experience what it is you desire to accomplish or experience. It will also cause you to flee from scenarios and situations where you should take a stand. This type of fear will cause you to flee in the midst of the uncertain, the unsure or the unknown. This kind of fear is a hindrance and will ultimately hold you back from the life that you truly desire. The Bible has hundreds of scriptures telling us not to have this kind of fear. This is the kind of fear that I want to see displaced at the core of your life. I want you to be able to say, *"I Was Afraid of That!"* That's right, past tense. But, I also want you to remember that not all fear is unhealthy.

The other common and basic word for fear in the Bible is *yirah*, which deals primarily with awe and respect. This type of fear keeps us safe from consequences. It's a healthy fear. It also carries with it a sense of reverence and worship. This word carries with it the sense of knowing God and His loving kindness, while understanding the depth of His character, stature and existence. It understands that the characteristics of God define who He is and it also realizes the importance of obedience and Lordship to an almighty, powerful and sovereign Creator. This kind of fear will establish the balance of awe and respect with allegiance and worship.

Out of some ten Hebrew nouns and eight verbs that are regularly translated "*fear,*" "*to fear,*" "*to be afraid,*" and similar words or phrases, only one of each is commonly used in the Old Testament and they both spring from the root-suffix "yr" and from the nouns being "yira" or "mora" and the verb "yare". However, the New Testament uses the words *phobos* and *phobeo* almost exclusively as a noun and verb, respectively, and these are the terms consistently used by the Greek Old Testament, the Septuagint, as well.

The fundamental and original idea expressed by these terms covers a semantic range from mild uneasiness to stark terror, depending on the object of the fear and the circumstances surrounding the experience. In time, however, fear of God or of manifestations of the divine became a subcategory of fear in general and thus it developed a profound theological significance that was pervasively attested to throughout the Bible. While the normal meaning of fear is dread or terror, it is also retained in the theological use of the terms. However, a special nuance of reverential awe or worshipful respect becomes the dominant notion.[1]

Now here's an interesting side note that I want to point out in regard to both the origin of fear and the defining

Chapter 2: Fear Defined

of the word fear. In Genesis, Adam said, "I heard Your voice in the garden, and I was *afraid* because I was naked; and I hid myself." The word afraid there is "*yare*", which has a myriad of meanings, both in theory and in thought. It would have described how anyone being afraid for the first time might have felt. It wasn't just terror or uncertainty that would have been felt, there would have also been a sense of awe and reverence. I believe Adam would have felt fear in the sense of uneasiness and anxiousness, but at the same time he would have been aware of the enormity and beauty of God, creating an awe and worship of His Creator in the midst of an uneasy fearful anxiousness.

FIGHT, FLEE OR FACE IT

So again, what is fear and how do we define it? VeryWellMind.Com has this to say about fear: [ii]"Fear is a natural, powerful, and primitive human emotion. It involves a universal biochemical response as well as a high individual emotional response. Fear alerts us to the presence of danger or the threat of harm, whether that danger is physical or psychological. Sometimes fear stems from real threats, but it can also originate from imagined dangers. Fear can also be a symptom of some mental health conditions including panic disorder, social anxiety disorder, phobias, and post-

traumatic stress disorder (PTSD). Fear is composed of two primary reactions to some type of perceived threat. Those reactions are: biochemical and emotional.

Biochemical Reaction[iii]

Fear is a natural emotion and a survival mechanism. When we confront a perceived threat, our bodies respond in specific ways. Physical reactions to fear include sweating, increased heart rate, and high adrenaline levels that make us extremely alert.[iv] This physical response is also known as the "fight or flight" response, with which your body prepares itself to either fight or flee. This biochemical reaction is likely an evolutionary development. It's an automatic response that is crucial to our survival.

Emotional Response[v]

The emotional response to fear, on the other hand, is highly personalized. Because fear involves some of the same chemical reactions in our brains that positive emotions like happiness and excitement do, feeling fear under certain circumstances can be seen or felt as fun, like when you watch an action movie or ride a roller coaster. Some people are adrenaline seekers, thriving on extreme sports and other fear-inducing thrill situations. Others have a negative reaction to the feeling of fear, avoiding fear-inducing situations at all

Chapter 2: Fear Defined

costs. Although the physical reaction is the same, the experience of fear may be perceived as either positive or negative, depending on the person and how they perceive what they are experiencing.

Symptoms[vi]

Fear often involves both physical and emotional symptoms. Each person may experience fear differently, but some of the most common signs and symptoms include:

- Chest Pain
- Chills
- Dry Mouth
- Nausea
- Rapid Heartbeat
- Shortness of Breath
- Sweating
- Trembling
- Upset stomach

In addition to the physical symptoms caused by fear, people may experience psychological symptoms of being overwhelmed, upset, feeling out of control, or even a sense of impending death.

Here's the deal, no matter how you define it, nothing can hold you back from reaching your full potential in

life quite like fear. Fear can limit your success, stunt your progress and keep all your hopes and dreams far from reach. Whether it is the fear of trying something new, the fear of going after something you want, the fear of making a fool of yourself, or something else you are afraid of, it can be enough to attack you from every side and angle, leaving you completely paralyzed and stifled at times. Don't allow fear to detour your destiny! If you let it, fear will dominate your thoughts, actions, and beliefs. You have to take captive those fear creating thoughts that can supplant the knowledge and love of God and focus on the reality of God's love and grace. Remember, *"Perfect love casts out fear."*

And, love has now been perfected by God through Christ. Therefore, I don't want to see you bound by a feeling or emotion that controls your life in a negative way. Not everything you feel is a fact! Your feelings and emotion must be challenged and kept in check. The good news is you don't have to give in to fear or let it control or ruin your life. But, in order to overcome it, you need to understand what it is, where it comes from and what it takes to face it. That's what this book is all about! As we continue to define fear, here are a few different types of fears that psychologists say exist in most of our lives.

Chapter 2: Fear Defined

Innate Fears[vii]

The first type of fears is universal, innate fears. Everybody has them on some level because they are born into us – in fact, most of them serve some kind of survival purpose. Innate fears are often centered around avoiding physical pain or death. Humans are born with a fear of spiders and snakes because we are wired to avoid objects that can harm us. No one ever taught you not to fear these creatures. The same goes for being afraid of flying, heights, pitch-black darkness or scary animals. We are wired to understand that these things pose an inherent danger and aren't safe. As we evolve as humans, some of the fears evolve with us, mostly to protect us from real danger.

However, we can also adapt to these fears and even ignore them if we choose. That's why we're able to climb mountains, fly planes and have animals as pets. And, at the same time, these innate fears aren't likely to keep you from success. You aren't likely to cripple your career with your fear of spiders. So, instead of confronting these fears, you can continue adapting or avoiding, as most humans do. Although it is easier to avoid and adapt. I believe that it is better for you to overcome your fear instead of adapting or avoiding, that is, in most cases.

Identity Fears[viii]

The second set of fears has also developed with us as we have evolved. These are fears that have to do with your identity. Primarily, they manifest as fears of being judged by others. The fear of public speaking is a great example. At the root of it, you are worried you are going to mess up and embarrass yourself. Other people will see how incompetent you may be and you will lose their respect. The fear of being wrong or being rejected stem from the same place.

The fears around your identity aren't about physical pain or death like our innate fears. But, you can certainly feel the physical effects of identity fears. Imagining that you will lose the respect of your peers can actually hurt. It can raise your blood pressure, make you feel hot and agitated, make you cry, etc. The emotional and psychological pain that identity fears cause is real – but it doesn't actually put you in any grave danger.

What identity fears have in common is that they pose a threat to your standing in the community. It also effects how you do life with simple routine and normalcy. You want to have an established place in your peer group and society because you depend on others for companionship, support, survival, etc. Identity fears come from a feeling of not being accepted and being left alone to survive on your own.

Love and Connection Fears[ix]
The final class of fears are those related to love and connection. Although they serve a different purpose, they are really a subset of identity fears. You might fear being alone, being abandoned, or being rejected. Trust issues show up in this category, too. You can fear commitment, which is often a way to protect yourself from ever having to experience rejection or feeling the pain of disappointment. You might also fear intimacy because you fear being hurt. The fears around identity and fears around love and connection can combine and become even more complex, like when a person doesn't believe they are worthy of love.

DON'T ALLOW FEAR TO HINDER YOU

Don't allow fear to hold you back any longer. The first step to stopping fear from holding you back is understanding what you are afraid of. Anything you fear usually would fall into one of these three categories. If you fear taking an action that you know you need to take, start by asking yourself what it is you really fear. The fears around your identity and love are generally the ones that prevent you from succeeding and being happy.

What will keep you from succeeding is never doing anything because of fear. Fear will hold you back from all significant accomplishments and victories. There is nothing worth doing that doesn't strike a little bit of fear in your heart; and, this applies to everything you do, including work, creativity, love, and just simply living life. There is nothing more satisfying in life than knowing that you tried your hardest and gave it your all. Don't let fear stop you from doing that.

Fear is your servant. If anything, it is here to prevent you from being harmed by real dangers. You cannot allow it to become your master and prevent you from taking the actions you need to take. If you do, it will keep you from success and happiness and it will rob you of your peace and joy. Fear is the number one obstacle you will face in life. It is the most difficult challenge you will ever be put to and the most important one to overcome. However, through love, grace, the Word of God and Christ, you have everything you need to conquer it!

Chapter 3

The Cause & Effect

WHAT WILL YOU DO

Someone said, *"What would you endeavor to do or be if you weren't afraid of failing or looking foolish?"* I believe that's a great question because I believe fear stops people from doing what otherwise they would strive to do or accomplish, that is, if they weren't afraid of failing or looking foolish. I also believe that if we took these two dilemmas, failing or looking foolish, out of the equation, we would eliminate most of the fears people have in regard to trying something new or different. I wonder how many developments, dreams, deals or discoveries were aborted because fear stopped those endeavors from becoming a reality. I want you to know: Failure is never final unless you stay down and don't get back up. And, the lesson is never lost if you learn from your mistakes and move forward!

I like to say it this way: *"Reach for the unreachable and in the process you may obtain what you thought was unattainable."* In other words, reach for the stars, swing for the fence, believe for the impossible and don't let fear stop you! Fear is a robber and a thief. Fear is a liar. Stop letting fear stop you. Take control today and defeat fear by doing whatever you want to do in spite of how you may feel. Courage doesn't mean that you're not afraid; it means that you respond in the midst of fear and uncertainty and accomplish more than you would have, if you would have never tried or believed to begin with. [x]*"It's better to have tried and failed than to live life wondering what would have happened if you wouldn't have tried."*

MIND MATTERS

Sometimes it's just a matter of mind over matter and the Spirit over the flesh. You may be afraid, but sometimes you have to do it anyway. You have to say it anyway! You have to believe it anyway! You have to try it anyway! You have to risk it anyway! If you never take the chance, you will never see the result or have the experience of conquering what has limited you for so long. I pray a newfound boldness will empower you. I pray a renewed courage will give you the audacity to rise up and do what you have for so long desired to try, to say or to accomplish. I want to see fear displaced at the core of your life so that you can say, *"I Was Afraid of That!"* That's right, past tense.

Chapter 3: The Cause & Effect

It all begins and ends in your mind. Your mind is where the battle begins and it is where it will end. Your mind helps manage what you magnify. That's why Paul in Philippians 4:8 tells us this: *"Whatever things are true, whatever things are noble, whatever things are just, whatever things are pure, whatever things are lovely, whatever things are of good report, if there is any virtue and if there is anything praiseworthy—meditate on these things."* You can't determine what happens, but you can control how you respond and you can control what you allow to dominate your thought life. Robin Sharma says, [xi]*"The mind is a wonderful servant but a terrible master."* You will either master your mind, or your mind will master you. Your mind will dictate your motivation and it will determine your movement toward what you desire to experience.

Your mind is the control center where everything is experienced and understood. You have a body that is a shell that houses your Spirit and soul. Your Spirit comes from God and is renewed when you are Born Again. Your soul is your mind, will and emotions. So you are body, soul and Spirit. Your soul realm is where you process your experiences and it's where you produce your expressions. Your mind has two primary functions: remembering and imagining. Your mind remembers and it imagines; it has a memory and it has an imagination. Thus, you can see how fear activates itself through your memory and imagination by *remembering* an unpleasant experience or by *exaggerating* it. Your memory will keep reliving an experience and your imagination will exaggerate it. That's why the Bible tells us to cast down arguments and to take every thought captive that exalts itself against the knowledge and love of God. You can't control every thought that goes through your mind, but you can control what you meditate on and you can take control of your thoughts before they take control of you.

Your mind has the ability to either minimize or magnify what you think, feel, sense or experience. Your brain is the control center for the gathering of all sensory information that is processed for you to experience or express. You can't control everything you experience, but you can control what you magnify. The longer you allow your mind to meditate on something that is creating fear, the greater the opportunity for that experience to magnify will increase. You have the power to tell your mind what to minimize and what to magnify. God has NOT given you a spirit of fear – but He has given you a sound mind!

Chapter 3: The Cause & Effect

That's the foundational scripture for this book and it is found in 2 Timothy 1:7 – *For God has not given us a spirit of fear, but of power and of love and of a sound mind.* Let's look at this verse and start at the beginning. If you have a spirit of fear, God did not give it to you. Now, I do want to say I believe you have God given instinctual fears that can be healthy and provide protection. But, a spirit of fear that torments or steals your joy or peace, is not from God. The Greek word for spirit in this verse is *pneuma*. I want to point out two major meanings of this word – the rational soul and the mental disposition.

In other words, when the scripture tells us that God DID NOT give us the spirit of *fear*, it's saying that He did not give us a (disposition) – '*prevailing tendency of fear*' or (rationale) – '*an agreeable reason to be afraid.*' Instead, He gave us power, love and a sound mind. The passage says *He's not given us the spirit of fear, but of power and of love and of a sound mind.* Did you get that? He didn't give us the spirit of fear, but He gave us the spirit of: power, love, and a sound mind. He gave us the mental disposition of power, the mental disposition of love and the mental disposition of a sound mind. He gave us a rational soul (the agreeable reason) of power, of love, and a sound mind.

Let's look at each of these attributes He gives us. He gives us the spirit of **POWER** (*dunamis*) – *miraculous, abundant, dynamic power*. In other words, He gives us a powerful ability that is more than enough to conquer fear. He gives us the spirit of **LOVE** (*agapē*) – *a strong affectionate brotherly love; a love feast; a love that is shared mutually with one another*. In I John 4:18 it says: "There is no fear in love; but perfect love casts out fear." In other words, love has been perfected among us in God through Christ and He gives us that spirit of His love to empower us to war against those things that intimidate us and cause fear in our lives. He gives us the spirit of **A SOUND MIND** (*sōphronismos*) - *an admonishing or calling to soundness of mind, to moderation and self-control*. Did you get that? He gives us the spirit and power to moderate and exercise self-control in regard to what our mind magnifies concerning fear.

INTERCONNECTIONS

This chapter is entitled: *Cause-and-Effect*. A cause-and-effect relationship is when something occurs that makes something else happen. This goes hand in hand when it comes to experiencing the emotion of fear. When you hear a loud noise in the other room, you become afraid of what it is, or, what might be

Chapter 3: The Cause & Effect

happening. The noise is the cause; the emotion of fear is the effect. Cause-and-effect allows you to make inferences and reason about things that happen around you. Causality is the relation between the cause and its effect. It helps us understand simple things like "If I don't do this, then this could happen." which in turn could create or cause fear. It could be something as simple as, "If I don't study for the test, I could fail the class." These realities could produce either a healthy or unhealthy fear in one's life.

In regard to cause-and-effect scenarios, cause is the thing that makes the other things happen, and effect is the result. Cause is the "why" something happened and effect is "what" happened. There are many things that cause and or create fear in an everyday life situation. Cause is the reason; effect is the result. The word cause is defined like this: a reason for an action or condition; something that brings about an effect or result. The word "creates" is defined like this: *to bring into existence; to produce or bring about by a course of action or behavior; to produce or design through an imagination.*

My point with the cause-and-effect theory is that fear is usually triggered by something. Therefore, the cause is the reason for the fear and the actual experience of fear is the effect. *"That scared me"*, or *"I was afraid!"* The cause-and-effect theory can take on many forms. Your memories, experiences and imagination also play a huge role in what you experience in regards to the emotion or feeling of fear itself.

What you remember as being unpleasant or as an unwelcome experience can trigger fear before what's being sensed is even experienced. Your past experiences of what you felt or remember can leave a lasting impression that can retrigger the same feeling in your new or current situation. And, what doesn't exist in reality, your mind can think up, or make up, creating a false reality that in turn, produces fear, which in actuality, shouldn't even exist to begin with. Your imagination as they say, *"can play tricks on you!"*

Your senses are another area that is responsible for you experiencing fear. As a reminder, the five human senses are: 1. Sight 2. Smell 3. Hearing 4. Touch 5. Taste. Each of these sensory attributes can connect you to the feeling or sense of being afraid. In my opinion, taste would be the least influential in this matter of creating fear unless, you were afraid something was going to burn your mouth or make you sick at your

Chapter 3: The Cause & Effect

stomach. Anyway, I would also say that the two greatest senses that would create fear would be sight and hearing. One of the first things we do as humans when we see something that frightens us is we close our eyes. And, when it's 'out of sight', it's 'out of mind.' That's right, the fear diminishes. What about hearing? Have you ever been watching a scary or suspenseful movie or a Netflix drama and been scared? Try turning down the volume and see what happens. I'll tell you what will happen; your fear level will drastically drop or it will completely go away. When the sound is no longer present and active for you to hear, the feeling you are experiencing will no longer exist. Fear subsides when the sound that was driving the fear disappears. Your senses many times determine what you do or don't experience.

Fear is caused by many variables. However, fear itself causes and creates many scenarios, emotions and dilemmas as well. Fear can cause *anger, illness and division.* It can make you mad, make you sick, and it can even cause you to choose sides. Fear can cause *procrastination, confusion and doubt.* It can make you put off what you should do, and it can make you disoriented to the facts. It can also make you question what you're doing or question if what you're doing is

I Was AFRAID of That!

worth the effort. Fear can cause *prejudice, uncertainty and hesitancy*. It can make you prejudge someone, some thing or some truth. It can make you unsure and it can cause you to become reluctant to try anything. Fear can cause indecision, sorrow and regret. It can cause analysis paralysis, making it difficult to make a decision. It can also magnify sadness and it can make you sorrowful for what you did or didn't do, all because of how it caused you to react or respond.

Fear will always attach itself to doubt and delusions. Again, you cannot control everything that happens to you or control every thought that enters your mind; however, you can control how you react and what you dwell on. Fear will cause you to **not** act upon what you truly desire all because you are not certain of the outcome. What I believe this creates in many cases is frustration, regret and the desire to give up. Don't give up and don't let fear dictate your experiences. Don't become so fearful in the present moment that you forfeit your future. If fear weren't an issue in your life, would many of the things we are talking about be an issue anyway? The answer to that question in many instances would be, probably not! Therefore, it's time to displace fear at the core of your life, so you can say, "I Was Afraid of That!" That's right, past tense.

Chapter 4

No More Intimidation

COVERED

The first time we have a record of the word *fear* being mentioned was in Genesis, the book of beginnings and the first book of the Bible. The first time fear was experienced and expressed by anyone was by Adam, the first of all creation. But, we have already established that in the introduction of this book. We also talked about how God showed up and was faithful to Adam and Eve when they were most vulnerable and afraid. It was only them and God; no one else could imagine or interpret fully what they may have been thinking or feeling at the time fear was first experienced. However, I believe the fear that they were experiencing undoubtedly included both a sense of terror and of awe.

As a matter of fact, I can imagine them having a sense of both terror and awe inclusively. It would have been a terrifying awareness of what they had just done, and a disheartening fear that had been awakened because innocence had just been stripped from their *virtuous* identity. But, at the same time, I'm sure that they would have had a real sense of awe and wonderment of their new found reality of who God truly was, as well. He was their maker and creator, their companion and friend. He was also Holy, righteous and just, the One who was and is, and is to come. God was the One who has been and always will be, the One who existed before their existence and the One in whom everything exists – by Him, in Him, and because of Him, including them!

I believe in this first account we have of fear, there was undoubtedly a plethora of emotions and feelings that were being experienced by Adam and Eve, the first of all creation. Could you imagine? Innocence was their only experience or expression, that is, up until this point. Adam was created in the image of God. He was formed into His likeness and God breathed life into his nostrils. Adam became a living being, a living being that walked in a harmonious fellowship with His creator in an environment that was created specifically for him. But now, in a moment, everything was lost. And now, all had to be restored. Adam and Eve were hiding in fear, but God was seeking their whereabouts in love.

Chapter 4: No More Intimidation

The fear that they were experiencing had to be overwhelming to say the least. They would have seen themselves in an entirely different light because of what they had done, and I'm sure they were seeing God in an entirely different light as well. Their perceptions and conceptions would now be forever tainted. And, their capacity for comprehension would never be the same. Fear changes everything. It changes the way we view reality, it changes the way we see ourselves, and it changes the way we see others. But, fear doesn't change God. That was good news for Adam and Eve. And, that is good news for you and me!

The same God who created them and walked with them in the garden in an unhindered relationship was now questioning where they were. A God who knows everything, knew where they were. But, where they were was connected to what they had done. So, when they heard the question, it was not only a reminder of what they had done. It was also an emotional experience of fear that had never been experienced up until this point. Again, could you imagine the feeling that must have overwhelmed them when they heard the whisk of His movement and the footfall of His steps in the garden? I wonder what they thought when they heard His voice utter the words, *"Where are you?"* Can you imagine the range of emotions that were experienced: the guilt, the shame, the doubt, and the overwhelming sense of intimidation and fear that must have gripped them in this *unthinkable* moment?

The had the awareness of now knowing the righteousness and holiness of God, the One Whom they had just disobeyed. This was the God who made them and gave them everything that they had and for that matter, everything that was good. But now, their eyes were opened to a whole new reality. They were now aware of their own nakedness and they were afraid. Therefore, they clothed themselves with fig leaves and hid in the trees because they heard the sound of The Lord, moving in the Garden. Wait a minute! Isn't that what we still do? When we hear something that is intimidating or frightening, we take cover and we hide.

Anyway, they hid. And then they sewed together fig leaves and made a covering for themselves. They tried to do for themselves, what only God could do. When you are afraid, or feel endangered, it's ok to hide. However, it is not ok to hide from God. Don't try to do for yourself what only God can do! They covered themselves with leaves, but it was God who made

Chapter 4: No More Intimidation

tunics of skin and covered them. They were hiding from the only One who could help them. Even worse, they hid in the very thing in which they had disobeyed God, the trees. And then, they justified what they had done by playing the blame game. You see when you are afraid, especially of being found out or being wrong: (1) You will hide, (2) You will justify and (3) You will project blame. That's what Adam and Eve did. They projected blame, they justified, and they hid in fear.

They hid because they were afraid of what would happen next. They covered themselves with the fig leaves they had sewn together by themselves, for themselves. Yet, like us, only God in His love, mercy and grace can truly cover us with His very own provision. Therefore, He made tunics of skin and clothed them. He covered them after He had set in motion the consequences for their disobedience. But, He showed His redemptive purposes when He clothed them with something that was warm, sustainable and lasting. And then, He put a Cherubim with a flaming sword swirling in every direction at every angle, so that Adam and Eve would not be lost in this condition eternally. Here's what I'm trying to say, if you're afraid and wondering if God will receive you or not, don't be, because He will. He came to seek and save that which was lost. You have no reason to fear! Your creator and maker is a loving God that will come to you in your times of fear and desperation.

Also, let's not forget, the Lord is not afraid to talk about what you and I are afraid to talk about. As a matter of fact, He dealt with the very things that were causing Adam and Eve to hide in fear. The Lord engages in a pointed conversation with them, asking them questions about what had just taken place. And, after a lengthy dialogue of questions and answers, came a somewhat extensive list of consequences for their disobedient actions that had just taken place. He talked about it and dealt with the issues at hand. He spoke the truth, but He did so in love through grace. Fear is reversed when truth is revealed in love.

AWE, REVERENCE, DREAD AND TERROR

The Bible tells us in I John 4:18-19 that perfect love casts out fear, because fear involves torment. It also says that the one who fears has not been made perfect in love. And, it concludes by saying that we love Him because He first loved us. God always makes the first move and sometimes that is the most mature thing anyone can do. The Greek word for *perfect* in I John 4 is: *teleios*. This word has many meanings and one of them is maturity. Sometimes you may need to be mature enough to face your fears and face the facts and deal with what needs to be dealt with. If you don't, there will always be a fear of what might happen or take place if what you're dealing with is not addressed. Don't live in torment! Pray and ask God for the courage to overcome your fear and to deal with what needs dealt with, in a mature and loving manner, so that you can get on with your life.

Now, before we move on, let's don't miss the beauty of this picture in regards to Adam and Eve. Here it is: God showed up! He showed up for Adam and Eve and He will show up for you and me. He showed up and kept his appointed time of fellowship with them. He was doing what He had always done, and they had been doing what they shouldn't have been doing. He was where He always had been, and they were hiding in fear. He was seeking a relationship and they were seeking isolation. Yet, in spite of all of their charades, God showed up and sought them out. You see, their sin and disobedience didn't change God, it changed them. And, in your sin, disobedience and fear, God will show up for you too. Therefore, there is no reason to live in turmoil, torment or fear.

I Was AFRAID *of That!*

Our sin, our fear and our uncertainty doesn't change Him or keep Him away. It changes us, but He still shows up. He shows up and He covers you with His love, power and strength that will help you conquer the very fear that is trying to conquer you. This is the very fear that is causing you to hide and isolate yourself from God and from others. God's plan is for relationship and there is no greater hindrance to a relationship then fear and isolation. That's why when our fear tries to cause us to hide and isolate, God shows up in His mercy and grace and He covers us in His love and peace! Thank God we are covered, and continually being covered in an eternal promise that becomes an internal realty that doesn't change according to external circumstances. He demonstrates His perfect love to us and that perfect love casts out fear!

Now, we've talked a lot about fear being mentioned in Genesis for the very first time. However, the first time the word fear was mentioned in the New Testament was in Matthew when the Angel of the Lord showed up to Joseph and said, *"Don't be afraid to take Mary to be your wife because the child in her womb is of the Holy Spirit."* And, it is mentioned again in Luke when the Angel of the Lord showed up to a young virgin girl named Mary. She was the one chosen to carry the

Chapter 4: No More Intimidation

promised Messiah, Jesus. It's interesting that the first time the emotion of fear was mentioned in the New Testament; it was correlated with the birth of Christ. And Christ, who would become the second Adam, ultimately abolished the power of fear in our lives. The eternal promises of God are fulfilled in Jesus and love has been perfected through Him. Therefore, we have no reason to fear!

Mary, the mother of Jesus experienced fear when introduced with the idea of carrying the Christ child, the Redeemer of the world and of all mankind. She was troubled when the Angel of the Lord first appeared to her. So the Angel of the Lord said, "Do not be afraid." She would be the one that would carry Jesus, the Savior of the world, the second Adam, the One who would restore fallen mankind back to a redemptive state with God. Maybe God was trying to show us that there is no reason to be troubled or to be afraid, because everything that we would experience that would ever cause us to doubt or fear, would be covered by His redemptive purposes.

From the announcement of Christ's birth, to the resurrection of our living Lord, when the people who encountered the Lord or His messengers were troubled, perplexed, or afraid, they were always given an explanation that would clarify what was taking place and why. I believe the reason that this is so important is because when it comes to the basic fears that most of us experience in life, the underlying issue is usually trust. That's right, trust. What you fear the most usually reveals what you trust the least. But, here's the good news: you can trust a God who sees and knows. And when fear is introduced, God already has a solution to the problem you are faced with. Even when you don't know or can't understand, you can trust Him! He is a very present help in time of need and His presence will bring you peace and dissipate your fear. Fear is no match for His love!

What started with a disobedient Adam in a garden at the tree of the knowledge of good and evil, ended with an obedient Jesus in another garden on another tree which was a cross on a hill called Golgotha. What Adam sowed in sin and disobedience Christ sowed in love and righteousness. It seems when you are obedient and have done all that you know to do, there is no reason to fear. It also seems that when you are disobedient and have been doing what you know you shouldn't have been doing, there is a valid reason to fear. But in our fear, we can still come to God and receive His

Chapter 4: No More Intimidation

mercy and grace. Adam and Eve were afraid, but God covered them. Christ became the second Adam and because of this, you can be covered in His righteousness. Therefore, there is no reason to fear because love has been perfected among us and perfect love casts out all fear.

I believe the kind of fear that love casts out is a consistent hindering or debilitating kind of fear. However, I believe Adam and Eve and Mary and Joseph, and, for that matter, anyone who encountered the Lord or one of His messengers in the Bible, experienced fear as a result of their encounter. And, the fear that they would have encountered undoubtedly made for dual experiences. The reason I point this out is because I want you to see the dual expression of the experience connected with the emotion of fear. The two words we looked at early in chapter two that are mentioned in the Bible, one in the Old Testament and one in the New Testament both have a dual experience linked to them.

In the Old Testament one of the words used for fear is: *Yare*. And in the New Testament one of the words used for fear is *Phobeo*. Both of these words have two implications in regard to their form, expression and

I Was **AFRAID** *of That!*

experience. One implication would be *to revere, honor or respect,* or to even *stand in awe of.* The other implication is *to be afraid, to dread, or to be terrified. Yare* is the word used in Genesis 3, when Adam says, *"We were naked and afraid (yare) so we clothed ourselves and hid." Phobeo* is the word used in the New Testament when the angel of the Lord showed up to Mary and to Joseph and said, *"Don't be afraid (phobeo)!"*

When you see these two words used in scripture it could mean that the person was in total awe or reverence or in total dread or terror. Or, even better yet, both at the same time. The correlation of meanings between these two words are polar opposite, yet uniquely connected. And, I believe this is what Adam and Eve and Joseph and Mary were probably experiencing. I believe that they were experiencing awe and reverence, and dread and terror, maybe all at the same time!

There always seems to be a sense of *awe* mixed in, when it comes to the emotion of *fear.* And, with *awe* also comes *intimidation.* Nonetheless, I believe this has more to do with a sense of being overwhelmed, than it does with being frightened or tormented. In II Timothy

Chapter 4: No More Intimidation

1:7, it says, *"For God has not given us a spirit of fear (deilia - timidity), but of power and of love and of a sound mind."* Notice this is a different word in the New Testament that is being used for fear. This Greek word is *deilia*. This word is defined using three word: (1) timidity, (2) fearfulness and (3) cowardice. Timidity is the primary definer. Some translations of scripture even use the word timidity in place of the word fear in regards to this passage.

In this passage found in II Timothy 1:7, Paul reassures us that a fear that restricts us is not God's idea or plan for us. He tells us that God has not given us the spirit of fear, nor has He given us inabilities, hate or an out of control mind. But rather, He has given us assurance, power, love and a controlled mind. Now, let's look at the definitions of these three words independently, and see what they mean in regards to the kind of fear that God has not given us:

(1) **Timidity** - lacking in courage, boldness, determination or self-confidence.
(2) **Fearful** - inclined to fear: timorous: fearful and of a timid disposition.
(3) **Cowardice** - lack of courage or firmness of purpose.

I Was AFRAID of That!

Notice all three of these words that are used to define the Greek word *deilia* deal with timidity, lack of assurance or lack of confidence. However, II Timothy 1:7 says *"For God has not given us a spirit of fear (deilia), but of power and of love and of a sound mind."* With that being said, if you look at verse six, the verse that precedes this verse, Paul tells Timothy to stir up the gift of the Holy Spirit that he had received when Paul laid hands on him and prayed for him. Then, he shifts gears and reminds Timothy and us in verse seven, that God has not given us the spirit of fear (*deilia*), but of power and of love and of a sound mind.

I believe what Paul is saying is this: when you experience fear and begin to feel intimidated or lack confidence, stir up the gift that is in you, the gift of the Holy Spirit. The Holy Spirit will empower you to overcome fear and cause you to become confident, courageous and convinced, convinced that God is with you and that He is more than enough! God has given to those who believe and receive His Spirit. And the Holy Spirit is an active agent to help bring power, confidence, peace, courage and assurance when one is experiencing fear.

Chapter 4: No More Intimidation

Now back to II Timothy 1:7. Paul says God hasn't given you the spirit of fear (deilia). Therefore, if God didn't give you this kind of fear, then where did it come from? I believe this kind of fear originated and came from the first Adam. I also believe we learn and develop fears as we live and do life. Nonetheless, as I've said before, I also believe Jesus became the second Adam and He came to abolish debilitating fear and to give us His peace. I don't believe it is God's best for us to live with a debilitating fear (deilia). This is the kind of fear: (1) that causes you to lack confidence, (2) that causes you to lack courage, (3) that causes you to be cowardly. This kind of fear (*deilia*) creates: (1) intimidation, (2) timidity, and (3) a restrictive restraint. This kind of fear is designed to paralyze and limit. This kind of fear begins with intimidation and ends in limitation.

The Latin word for timidity is *timidus*, or *timere*, which means to *fear*. When you are timid, you are fearful. It's obvious that intimidation, timidity and fear are linked. To intimidate means to make timid, frighten or overawe; to restrain or subdue by awe or fear. Intimidation is caused from a seemingly threatening force or foe. Intimidation creates fear and timidity, but intimidation is not based on fact; it is based on perceptions and feelings. Before allowing yourself to be intimidated, ask yourself this question: *Is what I'm fearing based on fact or feeling?* You have a choice in what you allow to intimidate you. You have the power to control what you think. Your life is choice driven and you can't allow your mind to create an intimidation that hinders you or causes you to fear. Your mind is where all fear is experienced, and it is where all fear can be defeated. You are an overcomer and you have the power to overcome fear and intimidation. The power of the Holy Spirit will empower you, causing you to be a victorious overcomer in and through Jesus Christ who loves you!

If you know that God is with you then you have no reason to truly be afraid. In reality, there is nothing you will face or experience that is beyond his grasp or ability. The Bible is full of pictures that point to God and His faithfulness. Don't be dismayed, intimidated or afraid, God is with you! Joshua 1: 9 says, *"Have I not commanded you? Be strong and of good courage; do not be afraid, nor dismayed for the Lord your God is with you wherever you go."* Adam and Eve were afraid and God showed up and covered them and clothed them. Mary and Joseph were afraid, but God showed up and Mary delivered Jesus, the promised Messiah and Joseph gave Him the name Jesus.

Chapter 4: No More Intimidation

The Bible is full of stories of people who were intimidated and fearful and people who were not. The choice is yours! The ten *"other spies"* of' the twelve spies that were sent out to spy the promised land were intimidated by and fearful of the giants of the land, but Joshua and Caleb were not! Saul and his army were intimidated by and fearful of Goliath, but David was not! Again, intimidation and fear is perception based and you have the power to overcome what you think and how you are feeling, in regard to any intimidation that may be causing fear.

I Don't believe it is God's plan for you to struggle with timidity or lack in regards to courage, boldness, determination or self-confidence. I also don't believe it is His intention for you to be fearful or, be inclined to fear or have a timid and fearful disposition. And lastly, I don't believe it is God's design for you to function as a coward who lacks courage or firmness of purpose, or who is intimidated by situations or circumstances that you are well able to overcome. That's why I'm writing this book. I want to see you become enlightened and empowered, so that you can see any debilitating fear that you may be experiencing displaced at the core of your life!

For Adam and Eve, for Mary and Joseph and for anyone who is reading this right now. I don't believe that it is God's best for you to live with a fear that limits you. I want you to know that God is with you and He is for you! He sent Jesus to become the second Adam, so that you could be empowered to rise above your fear. I want you to know that, *"God has not given you the spirit of fear, but of power and of love and of a sound mind."* He has given you the power to be empowered by the Holy Spirit. His love will strengthen and empower you and His love will cause your mind to be sound and controlled because He is love and perfect love casts out fear.

SECTION II
Common Fears

Chapter 5

Fear of Rejection

YOU'VE ALREADY BEEN ACCEPTED

The first thing that I want to say about rejection is, although it is real, there is no reason to truly fear rejection. That's because you have already been accepted. I want that to sink in for a minute. Read that again! Did you get that? You've already been accepted. You have already been accepted by your redeemer, your maker and your creator. He knows you the best and He sees everything. He knows your weaknesses and He knows your strengths. He knows where you will excel and He knows where you will fail. He sees your good days and He sees you bad days. And, He still chooses you!

Many times when you fear rejection, you are really fearing being rejected by someone who doesn't really matter. You may even experience the fear of being rejected by someone you don't even know. Don't do that! Because here's the irony of fearing rejection; you are actually dealing with a dilemma that may or may not happen. The fear of rejection will cause you to

I Was AFRAID *of That!*

worry, doubt and second guess yourself. It will cause you to become insecure before there's a reason to be. The fear of rejection is real and personal. Being rejected is a personal pain that comes from not feeling accepted or approved. And it's a fear that will keep you from exploring new opportunities in life. If you allow the fear of rejection to control you, you will never try or do anything new or significant. If you allow it to dominate you, it will create insecurities that will cause you to insulate your emotions and isolate yourself from experiencing anything that's new or different.

Fear comes from many sources and it exists for a variety of reasons. However, I believe the main reason that the fear of rejection exists is because it stems from identity issues. And, if you have a tainted identity of yourself, it will produce a greater insecurity as well. Insecurities are one of the main reasons someone experiences fear, especially the fear of rejection. It's a fear that you won't be accepted for who you are or for what you have done. It's a fear that will hinder you and cause you to isolate and hide. The fear of rejection will create a stronghold of insecure isolation. But, I don't want to see that happen. I want you to rise above the fear of rejection. I want to see you conquer what is trying to conquer you! I want you to know that you are

Chapter 5: Fear of Rejection

already approved and that you have already been accepted. It's my desire that you will see yourself as God does and that you will find your true identity in Christ Jesus.

I've been praying this prayer lately, maybe you want to pray it too: *"Lord, help me to see myself as you do. Not as others do, but as you do. Many will try to see me through my past or through a moment in time that was less than desirable, but help me, too, see me as you do. Others may see me through eyes of prejudice or pride, but help me to see myself as you do. Help me to not see myself by what I do or don't do, but rather help me to see myself through what you've done for me and have freely given to me, by grace through faith. I am accepted. I am approved. I am blessed. I am loved. I am forgiven. And, I am whole. I thank you now, for this truth, may it become a reality for me. In Jesus name, Amen.*

Seeing the reality of how Christ sees you is crucial to creating and maintaining a healthy and productive identity. In the Gospel of Matthew there is a passage that contains a verse that says, *"This is my beloved Son in whom I am well pleased."* It's God the Father talking to His Son, Jesus. It's where Jesus was being baptized by John the Baptist and the heavens open and the Holy

I Was **AFRAID** *of That!*

Spirit ascends upon Him like a dove and a voice from heaven declares: *"This is my beloved Son in whom I'm well pleased."* The interesting thing about this verse is Jesus had done nothing yet in regard to miracles, or, at least, that we have a record of anyway. An exception might be the record we have of Him astounding the scholars as a little lad in the Temple. Anyway, you get my point. Jesus hadn't opened a blind eye, walked on water, fed five thousand, calmed a storm, caused the lame to walk or healed a physical condition yet! But nevertheless, He was the Son of God, The Son of man, and The One in whom the Father was well pleased.

With this story I am trying to reiterate the fact that God loves you. He loves you for who you are, not what you do or don't do. He loves you as a son or a daughter, whatever the case may be. You are His creation. You are made in His image. He knew you before you were born and He knit you together in your mother's womb. You are wonderfully and fearfully made. You were created for a purpose and designed with an intent in mind. You don't have to earn God's love and approval; you already have it. When others reject you, He accepts you. When others disapprove, He approves. He is for you, not against you. God told Jesus that He was His *Beloved* Son in whom He was *well pleased*. The word

Chapter 5: Fear of Rejection

"beloved" in this text means esteemed, dear, favorite, and worthy of love. The word *"well pleased"* in this text means to take pleasure in, to be favorably inclined towards, and to think good thoughts about. You are the *beloved* of God; in whom He is *well pleased*. This means that God, your redeemer, maker and creator, your heavenly Father- believes that you are a son or a daughter that He takes pleasure in. It means that He believes that you are worthy of love and That He is favorably inclined towards you. I pray you believe that and receive that, in Jesus' name!

Here's another story to illustrate my point about already being accepted. I love to watch a reality talent show called The Voice. The title describes the premise of the show. It's all about the voice! Not image, not looks, not demeanor, not stature, just the voice. The show begins with what is called the Blinds or the Blind Auditions. The judges are sitting in chairs that rotate with their backs turned away from the contestants while they sing. However, if a coach likes what they hear, they turn their chair declaring that they choose that contestant to be on his or her team. But then the judges have to wait. They have to wait until the artist finishes their song, to see if any of the other judges turn their chairs. After all of that, the contestant gets

to choose whose team they want to be on, if there is more than one chair that turns for them during their performance.

Now remember, what's so great about this moment is that, the decision is solely based on the contestants' voice and nothing else. And, in this scenario there is such an awe and shock factor that adds to the drama of this moment because the judge hasn't yet turned their chair and the judges can't see who or what the contestant looks like yet. So therefore, the thrill is in the chair turn itself. That's also because the celebrity judge who happens to be a musical celebrity themselves and the contestant, who is blindly auditioning, see each other for the very first time as their fate is being decided. Right away, there are so many analogies I could draw from this situation, but here are a few:

1. The judge turns his/her chair for one thing: the voice. God doesn't choose you because of image, looks, demeanor or stature, either. He chooses you because He loves you and you are His creation, created for His creative purposes.

2. Only one person has to turn his or her chair for a contestant to be in the game or on the show.

Chapter 5: Fear of Rejection

Many are looking for a voice to fill the void. They are looking for acceptance, not rejection. But I've got good news for you, Jesus became that One! He turned towards you in a moment of love on the cross and then God turned His back on Him so that He would never have to turn His back on you. You've already been accepted. You've already been chosen by Him.

3. Once the chairs are turned the battle for the contestant really begins. The judges all have a reason why the contestant should choose them. Once the singer realizes that they have been chosen, the battle truly begins. There are many voices vying for the performers. And there are many voices vying for you. However, there is only One who ransomed you and redeemed you. He is the One who has chosen you for who you are and for what you mean to Him. God made a way through Jesus that you may be accepted and not condemned.

You are accepted, not rejected! The Voice is a great example that proves this point through a real life scenario. However, the other thing they do on this show is that they cultivate an environment where people can excel and become more. They work on

weaknesses and they develop strengths. They create a culture that celebrates and encourages. If you desire to be more, you must get around people who pull the good out of you. Don't stay around people who pull you down to their level and feed your insecurities. This will cause you to isolate. Get around people who speak life and speak hope and speak faith! Environment matters! A fish can flop foolishly on the sidewalk, but swim beautifully in a stream. Get in environments that cause you to become more. Get around people that will help you develop your potential. You are accepted, not rejected… God already turned His chair, so to speak. But, nonetheless, you are His beloved child in whom He is well pleased. Believe it! He believes in you.

THE REALITIES OF REJECTION

I want you to know that rejection is a horrible thing. But, I also want you to know that being rejected by someone is not the worst thing that can happen to you either. As they say, it's not the end of the world. As a matter of fact, it could be just the beginning of something new, better or different. The key is for you to not let rejection produce remorse, resentment or an unhealthy reaction. Sometimes the very thing that you wouldn't choose is what God will turn around and use. He will use it for your benefit and for His Glory! Being

Chapter 5: Fear of Rejection

rejected could be the very thing that brings what's necessary and next for you. Rejection sometimes produces a redirection and, in the process, it can also provide protection while creating a promotion.

In a sense, David in I Samuel 16 was rejected by being overlooked by his father, Jesse. Jesse was showing off all of his sons, except for David. The youngest son, the shepherd boy, David, wasn't even in the house. He wasn't even invited to the *'anointing for kingship'* party! Jesse had not even considered him to be anointed by Samul to be the next king of Israel. The Lord sent Samuel to the house of Jesse to anoint the next king of Israel and Jesse brought every one of his sons in to be anointed as king, never considering David. It wasn't until Samuel finally asked Jesse, *"Do you have any more sons?"* that he replied, *"I have one more."* David was out back attending to his father's sheep. David may have been overlooked by his brothers and his father, but not by God.

Being overlooked always brings with it a sense of rejection. David was overlooked for certain. But, God knew who he was and He knew where he was the entire time. And, God knows who you are and where you are as well. In this passage, God had rejected Saul

as being king over Israel. And Jesse had overlooked his faithful and diligent son, David. What's even more interesting as you read this story in I Samuel 16, is that the Lord tells Samuel not to look at the sons of Jesse's stature or appearance. The Lord goes on to tell Samuel that *He doesn't see man as man sees man!* He says, *"Man looks at the outward appearance, but I look at the heart."* God sees what we can't see and He knows what we don't know. You may have been rejected by man, but that doesn't mean you can't be used by God! Whether it's in regard to you or someone else, we mustn't reject what God accepts or accept what God would reject.

David was overlooked and rejected by his dad and the incident happened in front of his brothers. But, he was also anointed as king in front of his brothers as well. God protected David because he wasn't even there to see what was happening. But, God allowed him to be anointed in front of everyone that did see what had happened. God may allow you to be promoted right in front of the very people that rejected you. When you are rejected, never seek revenge. Instead, allow God to be your vindicator. His ways and His timing are perfect! David didn't have to say anything. God did the speaking to Samuel and here's the passage in I Samuel 16:10-13:

Chapter 5: Fear of Rejection

¹⁰ Thus Jesse made seven of his sons pass before Samuel. And Samuel said to Jesse, "The LORD has not chosen these." ¹¹ And Samuel said to Jesse, "Are all the young men here?" Then he said, "There remains yet the youngest, and there he is, keeping the sheep." And Samuel said to Jesse, "Send and bring him. For we will not sit down till he comes here." ¹² So he sent and brought him in. Now he was ruddy, with bright eyes, and good-looking. And the LORD said, "Arise, anoint him; for this is the one!" ¹³ Then Samuel took the horn of oil and anointed him in the midst of his brothers; and the Spirit of the LORD came upon David from that day forward.

David was anointed king but continued caring for his father's sheep and ministering to Saul by playing his harp. Tending to his father's sheep was where God developed David's faith. And, it is also where David developed his skill. David didn't assume kingship immediately. Don't allow the delay of rejection to discourage you. Don't waste your wait! Whenever you are faced with rejection, or any kind of misfortune for that matter, ask yourself this: *what can I learn from this?* David learned that his God was faithful when a lion and a bear crossed his path and he killed them with his bare hands. He also learned to develop the skill of using a slingshot. You see, what you thought was going to destroy you is what God will use to develop you!

David's dad, who thought of him last in the lineup to be anointed king, sent him to the battlefield to take some

I Was **AFRAID** *of That!*

cheese sandwiches to his brothers and to King Saul who were fighting the Philistines. There was a giant from the Philistine camp named Goliath. He was huge and he was taunting them day and night. To make it even worse, Goliath was mocking their God. By now intimidation and fear had gotten the best of them and they now were fearing the worst. David came to the battlefield to bring cheese sandwiches to his brothers, but he ended up battling the giant and winning.

He didn't allow the rejection of being overlooked by his father or, the ridicule and the mocking of his brothers and King Saul to keep him from stepping up against the giant with just a slingshot and five smooth stones. He didn't stand down, he stood up! He's the only one that didn't call Goliath by his real name. He calls him instead, an *uncircumcised Philistine*. And David declares to him loudly, *"You come to me with a sword and a spear, but I come to you in the name of the Lord!"* David wins the battle by defeating Goliath and is ultimately crowned King because of it. He didn't allow rejection to defeat him; he allowed it to develop him. And you can do the same! The reality is, rejection only has the power that you allow it to have in your life. Don't allow it to defeat you, allow it to develop you!

Chapter 6

Fear of Failure

FAILURE IS NOT FINAL

The fear of failure is something about which I am all too aware. I truly believe that for me this was always rooted in perfectionism. I wanted to do everything perfectly and be good at everything I did or I didn't want to do it at all. Therefore, if I couldn't do it perfectly, I would define that as less than perfect or a failure. I was also afraid of looking foolish. Of course, when you get to the bottom of being afraid of looking foolish, it is really rooted in pride. I believe this is also an issue for anyone who deals with timidity as well. I also didn't want to be disappointed. And mostly, I didn't want to disappoint anyone else. Failure is disappointing. What you had hoped would be the outcome, isn't. What you desired to be the result, is not even in the equation. Failure is a personal dilemma and the fear of failure is as well. The fear of failure is something that can cause a crippling self-doubt while producing a fear to fail that is based on the ridicule you may face from others after a failure.

I Was **AFRAID** *of That!*

In my adolescent years, it seemed like everything I did was based on the fear of being judged on my performance- whether it was how I lived my Christian life, how I dressed, how I played an instrument or how I delivered a message. Now, I'm not saying that for you to feel sorry for me. I'm just saying, for me, you, or anyone else, if there is a scorecard being held up in front of you to perform or there is an ultimatum or declaration that is rooted in fear, you will be bound to freeze up and will definitely forfeit trying something you could fail. The fear of failure will keep you from trying something that you may succeed at doing. The fear of failure, much like the fear of rejection, is a drawn conclusion before the results are concluded. But what I want you to know is: failure is not failure, unless you don't learn from the experience.

Therefore, if you learn from the experience, it's no longer considered failing. That's because all was not wasted, since an experience was gained to draw from later. And, failure is never final if you get back up and try again! If success is your goal, then you have to keep trying until you succeed. When you have an experience where you didn't succeed, it's an opportunity to try it again, with the understanding that this time you know what to do or what not to do. The thing you don't want

Chapter 6: Fear of Failure

to do is to give up in defeat, all because you allowed discouragement to get the best of you. You can't internalize failure and ever expect to learn from it or overcome it. There's nothing wrong with owning failure, but there is something wrong with allowing failure to own you. Don't be afraid of failing! Just like the fear of rejection, it's not the end of the world. Dr. Henry Cloud says that the only problem with failure is how most of us perceive it. Here are some perspectives in regard to failure:

> "I have missed over nine thousand shots in my career. I've lost almost three hundred games. Twenty-six times I was trusted to take the game winning shot and missed. I have failed over and over and over. And that's why I succeed!"
> - Michael Jordan

> "Failure is the tuition we pay for success."
> - Walter Brunell

> "Only those who dare to fail greatly can ever achieve greatly."
> - Robert F. Kennedy

Here's What Dr. Henry Cloud Says:

1. You make it **PERSONAL** by saying, "What is wrong with me!"
2. You make it **PERVASIVE** by saying, "I can't do anything right!"

3. And then you decide it's **PERMANENT** by saying, "This will never change or get better!"

Here's What Failure Will Do:
- It will keep you tied to the past.
- It will keep you bound by regret.
- It will keep you from trying one more time.
- It will keep you from believing in yourself.

Failure only has the power in your life that you allow it to have. It can produce a negative result or it can produce a positive outcome, depending on how you view what has happened. Don't allow the fear of failure to defeat you any longer. Just because something failed in the past, that doesn't mean it has to fail this time or in the future. Don't allow regret to turn into remorse all because you failed. Don't regret the very thing that taught you a lesson. Be grateful that you gained experience and that you matured in a way that you couldn't have matured any other way.

Don't allow failure to create self-doubt. Have faith and confidence in a God who created you and made you in His image for a purpose. Don't allow failure to affect your worth, value or identity. Believe in yourself, God does! And, it's not over until He says it's over! Fear is not fatal and fear is not final. You can't let it deter you

Chapter 6: Fear of Failure

and you can't let it define you. You must overcome the fear of failure before it causes you to succumb to the outcome that you truly desire. Remember, fear is never final, unless you allow it to be.

When I think of failure from the perspective of being a preacher, I often think of the disciple Peter. Not that he was a failure, because I believe that he was far from it. But, I also believe that his life was a contradiction to what he would have fundamentally chosen. And, that what he desired to do and what he truly experienced or accomplished was less than what he truly intended or ultimately expected. However, sometimes what appears as failure is not failure and sometimes what looks like a setback is actually a setup. Remember this, you will never fail if you never try. Peter was someone who wasn't afraid to try! He would risk the humiliation and do it anyway.

Sometimes you'll have to do it anyway. You will have to respond and take a risk in spite of how you feel. There are many times when you will have to do things even if you are afraid. You may have to risk rejection if you are ever truly going to succeed. Peter said he would never forsake Christ, but he did! But, he also wasn't afraid to declare that Christ was the Lord when Jesus asked,

I Was AFRAID *of That!*

"Who do you say I am?" What if Jesus would have said, *"That's not the answer I was looking for."* Peter wasn't afraid to fail. He took the risk of being wrong and came up with the right result in an answer that Christ was looking for. As they say, *"There's nothing to fear but fear itself!"* Doubt your doubts. Face your fear and take the risk. Failure is not final!

Peter exemplifies the "fail often" principle of life. We can all relate to him because he had great intentions but often messed up in dramatic fashion: (1) He offered advice to Jesus on how He shouldn't give up his life and Jesus called him Satan. (2) Another time he hopped out of the boat and walked on water before losing focus and then he sank like a 'rock'. (3) There was the time when he bravely defended Jesus, but cut off a guy's ear. (4) Then Peter failed "the mother of all failures" when he denied Jesus three times.

The full impact of these lessons didn't fully sink in until after the resurrection when Jesus forgave and restored Peter. That's not the way we reward failure, but God is different. Peter's life consisted of trying, failing, learning, adjusting and trying again. His "failing forward" is probably what contributed to God's decision to choose Peter as guest speaker on the "Day

Chapter 6: Fear of Failure

of Pentecost." Peter failed greatly, but he learned from his mistakes and tried again. Then he preached and led three thousand people to Christ and helped birth the New Testament Church!

Mark records the story of Peter denying Christ like this in Mark 14:66-72: *⁶⁶Now as Peter was below in the courtyard, one of the servant girls of the high priest came. ⁶⁷And when she saw Peter warming himself, she looked at him and said, "You also were with Jesus of Nazareth." ⁶⁸But he denied it, saying, "I neither know nor understand what you are saying." And he went out on the porch, and a rooster crowed. ⁶⁹And the servant girl saw him again, and began to say to those who stood by, "This is one of them." ⁷⁰But he denied it again. And a little later those who stood by said to Peter again, "Surely you are one of them; for you are a Galilean, and your speech shows it." ⁷¹Then he began to curse and swear, "I do not know this Man of whom you speak!" ⁷²A second time the rooster crowed. Then Peter called to mind the word that Jesus had said to him, "Before the rooster crows twice, you will deny Me three times." And when he thought about it, he wept bitterly.*

Proverbs 24:16 says, "For though the righteous fall seven times, they rise again, but the wicked stumble when calamity strikes." The word *calamity* means *distress, adversity, misery and evil*. Don't fall to calamity! Rise up in faith and don't allow fear to create a stronghold of

procrastination paralysis. No matter how many times you fall, get back up again!

It was never God's plan for Peter to sit outside the gate and weep bitterly at the regret of failure. It was God's plan that Peter be restored and used by Him, that's why He asked him three times, *"Peter, do you love me?"* Three times he denied Him, and three times the Lord asked him, *"Do you love me?"* And Peter replied "yes" every time. It was God's plan that Peter would be restored and preach on the Day of Pentecost declaring the goodness of God and three thousand be added to the church that day. Failure is disappointing, but it doesn't have to be disqualifying. It was the devil's plan that Peter stay defeated. But it was God's plan that he would be restored. There's no failure bigger than God! And even if you do fail, He is ready to restore you. God will not reject you. He loves you. He is for you. Failure is not final. Therefore, there is no reason to fear it! Failure doesn't define you unless you allow it to, and failure is not failure unless you allow it to be. If you have failed, get up, learn, live and try again, again and again! There's no reason to fear failure, because failure is not final! Learn, get back up and try again.

Chapter 7

Fear of the Future

THE UNKNOWN IS NOT UNKNOWN TO GOD

As I began writing this book, we were on the precipice of a worldwide pandemic. And, today, as I'm writing this chapter, our country just finished voting in an election for the president of the United States and we still don't know the results. And what this means for so many is fear and uncertainty. No matter on what side of the political banner you may stand, the nation is divided. For one group, the current president, Donald Trump and Vice-President Mike Pence would be the answer and for another group, former Vice President Joe Biden and U.S. Senator Kamala Harris would be the ticket.

But, for those that stand on either side, if their candidate is not chosen, it might seem like the end of the world, or, at best, the worst thing that could have ever happened. It would paint a picture of an uncertain future, full of ideas and policies, that are less than desirable. It would appear for either side that no one wins and the future that would continue on or now be created, would not be what is desired from either side. In other words, if Biden and Harris would be elected, it would be a disappointing outcome and would appear to be an unwanted and uncertain future for those who support President Trump and Vice President Pence. And it would be vice versa for those who support former Vice President Biden and Senator Harris. It appears our nation is divided and this creates even more unrest and uncertainty.

There is so much uncertainty in regards to our world and what the future holds for us. There's the looming and continual COVID 19 global pandemic that includes wearing masks, limited gatherings and the continued social distancing recommendation of staying six feet apart from one another. There is corruption and deceit in society, politics and journalism. We are bombarded with political agendas, social injustice and societal unrest daily. We are plagued with acts that are a defilement and gross perversion, but that are currently being viewed as ok by many. There is so much unrest and uncertainty around the world today and many wonder if and when it will ever come to an end. But even in the midst of unrest and uncertainty, we can trust an unknown future to a God who knows and sees

Chapter 7: Fear of the Future

everything! Don't allow a fear of the future to produce a stronghold of unknown uncertainty.

With that being said, when times are uncertain, unknown, unexpected or unexplainable it seems that common clichés and timeless truths are sometimes frustrating to hear and even more annoying to consider. Nonetheless, common clichés are often true and timeless truths never change. Therefore, no matter who is elected president of the United States, God is still on His throne in heaven! He still loves, saves, heals, delivers and helps. When the future is uncertain for you and me, it is never more certain for God. He is never wondering or doubting and He is never faced with something that is beyond His comprehension, ability or knowledge. There is a common cliché that says, *"I don't know what the future may hold, but I know Who holds the future."* Although this is a common cliché it's still true. And, it's very timely as well.

God is the One who is and was and is to come. He is faithful, righteous, just and Holy. He is the one Who created the heavens and earth and the One who sits on His throne in Heaven. He is the one who shut the mouths of lions, parted the Red sea, and opened the womb of Sarah. He is everlasting to everlasting, He is

I Was AFRAID of That!

the Alpha, Omega and the beginning and the end. He is the One who stepped out on nothing and created everything. He is the fourth man walking in the fire and He is the one that will walk you through your uncertainty! God is ever present and always concerned, but He is never taken by surprise or wondering what to do next. And He is faithful! This statement is true not only in regard to a presidential election or COVID 19, but in every area of our lives.

The Lord sees all things and He is capable of anything. He establishes our end from our beginning and our beginning from our end. Whenever we establish or begin something, we would start at the beginning because it's the only reference point obtainable for us. However, God is omnipresent and He sees the beginning of time and the end of time, all at the same time! Therefore, He goes to the end of my life and establishes it. Then He comes back to the beginning and walks with me back through it to the end. He empowers, keeps, helps and sustains. The Lord knew us before we were and He knit us together in our mother's womb. He will never leave us nor forsake us, but He will be with us to the end. That's why we can trust an unknown future to a known and proven God. He is all knowing and He is all powerful. The unknown is not unknown to God. He knows, even when you and I don't know. That's why you can trust the unknown future to an all knowing and faithful God!

YOU CAN BE CERTAIN

What I've learned in living my life thus far is this: nothing is for certain, except for God. And what I thought for certain was the worst thing that could possibly happen, usually wasn't. I've also found that what I thought might happen, didn't always happen and what I thought would never happen, sometimes did. When you have a fear of the future, it's a fear of the unknown because the future is not fully known to anyone, except for God. There are things you plan for and there are things that will take you by surprise. But, don't allow the fear of the future to rob you of your joy right now. And, don't allow it to steal your peace in moments that you may not regain. Today is all you have, tomorrow is promised to no one. Therefore, don't allow a fear of the future to rob you of the blessings that are meant to be experienced today.

Listen to what Jesus tells us in Matthew 6:25-34:
[25] *"Therefore I tell you, do not worry about your life, what you will eat or drink; or about your body, what you will wear. Is not life more than food, and the body more than clothes?* [26] *Look at the birds of the air; they do not sow or reap or store*

I Was **AFRAID** *of That!*

away in barns, and yet your heavenly Father feeds them. Are you not much more valuable than they? ^{27} *Can any one of you by worrying add a single hour to your life?* ^{28} *"And why do you worry about clothes? See how the flowers of the field grow. They do not labor or spin.* ^{29} *Yet I tell you that not even Solomon in all his splendor was dressed like one of these.* ^{30} *If that is how God clothes the grass of the field, which is here today and tomorrow is thrown into the fire, will he not much more clothe you—you of little faith?* ^{31} *So do not worry, saying, 'What shall we eat?' or 'What shall we drink?' or 'What shall we wear?'* ^{32} *For the pagans run after all these things, and your heavenly Father knows that you need them.* ^{33} *But seek first his kingdom and his righteousness, and all these things will be given to you as well.* ^{34} **Therefore do not worry about tomorrow, for tomorrow will worry about itself. Each day has enough trouble of its own.**

These are Jesus' very own words to us. He clearly says to NOT worry about tomorrow. Worry is an unhealthy concern that can cause torment and, in turn, produce fear. Could it be that Jesus was saying that there is no reason to fear the future, as long as you trust me? Isaiah 26:3 says, *"You will keep in perfect peace those whose minds are steadfast, because they trust in You."* In other words, when our minds are steadfast on God and His word and His ways, then we will have peace. But, when we focus on things that are unknown,

Chapter 7: Fear of the Future

uncertain or that are beyond our knowledge or control, we won't have peace and we will be dominated by fear. I truly don't believe that this is God's plan or His best intention for us. I believe it is His desire for us to not fear the future, but to trust in Him!

You can trust God! You may know this to be true, but I also know that when circumstances surround you that are unplanned and uncertain it can cause you to doubt. You can know something for certain, but when you are faced with something that is unexpected or that is uncertain, it can make you doubt what you already know. For example, before Jesus was betrayed, beaten and hung on a cross, He told His followers over and over again that He would rise from the dead. But when they were actually faced with an empty tomb, they began to doubt what they were seeing and they began to doubt what He had told them time and time again.

However, the Christian faith is defined by a triumph over fear and uncertainty. The scenario begins with a surrendered savior nailed to a bloody cross. It then unfolds into an empty bloody cross because Life had surrendered to Death and His body was taken down from the cross and clothed in grave clothes and laid in a tomb with a stone rolled in front of it. However, Life

I Was AFRAID *of That!*

ultimately conquered death and what we see at the end of this story is an empty tomb, with a risen Savior that lives. And Jesus is now making intercession for us, even as I type these very words. That's the foundation of the Christian faith and that's why you can trust an unknown future to an all knowing and faithful God!

In Jeremiah 29:11, it tells that God will give us a future and a hope. The future you are facing may be uncertain, but there is a future that God has planned for us called Heaven that is sure and certain. This is our future for all of eternity, if we've put our faith in Christ. It's a place where there is no more fear, no more darkness, no more dying, no more uncertainty, no more fear of an unknown future. In heaven the future is secure and complete, all at the same time. Heaven is our future hope, but that doesn't mean that we twirl our thumbs, bury our heads or freeze up in fear today. It means that we live our lives in hope every day. It means that although the future down here may be unknown, there is no reason to fear the future when we serve a God who sees and knows everything. You don't have to fear the future, if you trust in Him!

Chapter 8

Fear of Not Being Good Enough

SELF-IMAGE, STRENGTHS AND UNIQUENESS

Unworthiness, no doubt, is at the root of the fear of not being good enough. However, I believe the feeling of unworthiness is unnecessary, that is, if you focus on the right thing. Don't allow unnecessary unworthiness to become a mindset that creates a stronghold. Unworthiness is self-doubt. Doubting yourself is normal, but letting it stop you is a choice. You may never feel like you are good enough, especially if you focus on what you lack or if you focus on your shortcomings, rather than focusing on your obvious strengths and your uncommon uniqueness. Today I want you to know that no matter what your self-image or inward perceptions may be, you are good enough! You are good enough because you are God's creation, made in His image. Your value and worth are not determined by your own self-image or man's opinion. They are determined by God's love for you. He knew you before you existed and He sees you even now in this very moment of time. And He sees you as more than enough!

He sees your preexistence, your past, your present and your future all at the same time. And, in each moment of your existence, He sees you as being well able, more than capable and full of potential and possibilities. You are His creation and you are more than enough! You don't have to measure up to everyone else's standards. If you are in Christ, you are seen by God, through Him and by Him and that's enough. He is the perfect measure. He is the perfect standard and your identity is now found in Him! I want you to know that God doesn't make mistakes or create less than human beings. By His love and through His Grace He has made you more than enough!

Your own perception of who you are and the perspective of what others see will often affect how you feel. What you do and why you do it is often determined by how you view yourself or by how you feel about how others view you. However, I also believe that perspectives, perceptions, motives and for that matter, even forgone conclusions should be seen through the lens of how God sees you. You are His creation and He values what you do and who you are. The lens by which you view things will determine what you see. Whenever you feel *'less than'*, don't you ever forget that you are God's creation, created in His

Chapter 8: Fear of Not Being Good Enough

image. You are His workmanship, created for good works, which God prepared beforehand that you should walk in them. However, you won't walk in the fullness of what God has in store for you if you constantly fear not being good enough.

You have to view yourself as being positioned in Christ and loved by God to understand your true worth and value. Remember us talking about David in chapter four of section I? David was the shepherd boy and son of Jesse who was chosen by God to become king. I would say he probably had to deal with a fear of not being good enough, wouldn't you? Especially after dealing with the scenario of his father choosing all of his other brothers over him to be anointed king. When, in all actuality, God had already chosen him! You see it takes real confidence and integrity to have self-confidence when no one else sees or recognizes what you know or what God sees. However, I believe David found his sense of worth through knowing and believing that he was God's chosen and anointed man to become king.

I also believe that David developed and deepened a relationship with God while attending to his father's sheep on the back side of a mountain. And, I believe that the relationship that David developed with the Lord, in turn, developed him. I also believe that, because of this, David believed that he could conquer the giant, Goliath. Although the giant was taller, stronger and more experienced, David ultimately conquered him by putting his faith in God. God chooses to use ordinary people just like David and just like me and you to accomplish extraordinary feats. That's why it's vital for you to know who you are in Him! If you never conquer the fear of not being good enough, you will never have the courage to face what you fear and see that fear defeated.

God chose you! The value of something is seen by what someone is willing to pay for something. God sent Jesus to die for you. He gave His life for you. That's how much value He placed on your life. He gave His life so that you may have life and have it more abundantly. He loves you and He is for you; He is not against you. Now, before we go any further, I want you to know that this chapter is not just about building your self-confidence; it's also about building your God-fidence. That is, your confidence in who you are in God, through Christ Jesus.

Chapter 8: Fear of Not Being Good Enough

This book is about displacing fear at the core of your life and this chapter is about dealing with the fear of not being good enough. I don't want to see a lack of confidence or an overwhelming sense of unworthiness to keep you from being all that God has created you to be or designed you to do. The fear of your not being good enough or the fear of something you have done, not being good enough, has to, at some point, be met with the reality of how God sees you. This can't be about how you see yourself or how others see you, it has to be about how God sees you. That's the identity you need to embrace. That's the reality you need to rehearse and become familiar with. The identity of a new creation in Christ! God sees you as being saved, blessed, redeemed, restored, healed, and therefore, hopeful because you are more than an overcomer and conqueror in Christ Jesus. You are capable enough, strong enough, smart enough and equipped enough to accomplish whatever is set before you to accomplish.

COMPARED TO WHOM–COMPARED TO WHAT

You are more than enough, but you have to see it and you have to believe it! How others view you is not nearly as important as how you see yourself. And sometimes how we see ourselves compared to how others see us, is a sharp contrast. Let me illustrate: I

was teaching a group of people one night and began to share vulnerabilities and insecurities. So I began to bear my soul about how I really viewed myself through the lens of my own insecurities. After I had taught, some people started coming up to me and talking about the teaching and every one of them said, "You know what you said about yourself tonight?" I said, "Yes." And they said, "We didn't think any of those things about you and we don't see you that way when we look at you or think about you." In other words, what I felt through my vulnerable sincere insecurities, is not how anyone in that room that night saw me.

With David it may have been just the opposite in regard to his own self-image versus how others seemingly perceived him. I believe, ultimately, he saw himself as God saw him. Not as others saw him and probably not even as he saw himself, but I believe he saw himself as God did– strong and able! How others perceived him would have been less than what he appeared to be and indisputably lower than what he was capable of accomplishing. He killed a giant for crying out loud! Nonetheless, David's dad obviously perceived him as being too young to be the one chosen and anointed as king, let alone being the one to take down Goliath and, in the end, win the battle against the Philistines.

Chapter 8: Fear of Not Being Good Enough

You see, sometime after David had been anointed King by Samuel, his father sent him to the battlefield to take some cheese sandwiches to his brothers and to Saul, the leader of the army. This is where they were fighting Goliath and the Philistines. His brothers asked him why he came down there because they saw him as a little, inadequate, annoying, brother. Saul saw him as a kid amongst men and tried to put his own armor on him. Goliath was humiliated that David would even try to fight against him. Goliath even declared, *"What am I a dog that you a child would come after me with a stick?"* If David would have listened to everyone else's opinions, he would have never accomplished anything. But instead, he listened to an inner voice that told Him that his God was bigger and that he was more than able to conquer and defeat the giant that day, and he did!

David came to Goliath in the name of the Lord! There is a difference between arrogance and confidence and there's a difference between confidence and God-fidence. Arrogance points to one's self. Confidence points to one's faith and to one's God. Confidence is an assurance of who you are in Christ. God-fidence is your faith and confidence of who God is in you. David had faith and confidence in His God and David knew that his

I Was AFRAID of That!

God had faith and confidence in him. David knew that he was strong in God and David knew that God was strong in him. As a matter of fact, it changed how David saw the battle and it changed how he saw himself compared to Goliath.

It's amazing how your perspective can change, depending on how you see yourself in Christ. As a matter of fact, everyone else called Goliath, "Goliath". But David called him an uncircumcised Philistine. David saw him for who he was and saw himself for who he was in God. David didn't come to the giant in arrogance, he came to him with God-fidence. He said, "The Lord will help me defeat you. I will knock you down and cut off your head and I will feed the bodies of the Philistines to the birds and wild animals. Then the whole world will know that Israel serves a real God!" You talk about confidence. You talk about faith. You talk about courage. You talk about God-fidence!

David said, *"You come to me with a sword and a shield, but I come to you in the name of the Lord!"* Notice David didn't say, *"I came with a slingshot and five smooth stones, but I'm only going to need one!"* That would have been arrogance. Knowing that you are good enough isn't about arrogance, it's about confidence.

Chapter 8: Fear of Not Being Good Enough

Faith should build confidence. Faith is what or whom you believe in, but confidence is what gives you the courage to act upon what you believe. David had faith, but he also had confidence and courage.

You can have all the faith in the world, but if you don't have confidence you won't have courage and if you don't have courage you won't move in faith towards what you're trying to conquer or accomplish. You have to face what you fear in order to conquer what needs to be defeated. David conquered the uncircumcised Philistine that day, but he didn't do it by considering or comparing. He conquered the giant through faith and confidence in God and by realizing who He was through God's help and by His power. David didn't compare himself to the giant, he compared His God to the giant, and, with that, there were no more comparisons left.

I like to say it this way: *"Don't dare compare!"* Comparing usually leads to a critical spirit, arrogance, cynicism, or selfish pride. None of which are good. Nonetheless, there's no need to compare because you are uniquely and wonderfully made in the image of God. No one is like you and no one can do what you do or do it the way that you can do it. But here's the thing,

I Was AFRAID *of That!*

when you are faced with the fear of not being good enough, there is usually always an element of comparison involved that you will have to guard against and resist. Social media adds to this dilemma of comparison as well. The fear of not being good enough is fed by approval, self-esteem and contentment. Any and all of these attributes help contribute in regard to feeding or destroying your self-image.

Don't allow that to destroy you! Don't compare! Remember what God told Samuel when he was going to Jesse's house to anoint a king. He told him to not to look at the outward appearance, because God looks at the heart. Don't you do it either! Remember, there will always be someone better looking, stronger, richer or smarter, but there is also no one like you! You were uniquely and wonderfully made, created in the image of your creator. You were created with a purpose in mind and no can fulfill your purpose. No one can do what you do and no one can do it the way you can do it. So don't allow the fear of not being good enough keep you from trying what you need to do or from being who you were created to be. You are more than enough, in God and through Christ!

Chapter 9

Fear of Not Having Enough

Things You May Fear Not Having Enough of:
- Time
- Money
- Food
- Opportunities
- Friends
- Education
- Success

SHUTDOWNS, SHORTAGES AND STOCKPILES

Although I haven't mentioned much since I wrote about it in the introduction, nonetheless, we are still in the midst of the COVId-19 pandemic. As a matter of fact, some countries are going back on shutdown and the United States is still grappling over wearing masks, social distancing of six feet apart and limited social gatherings. We are actually celebrating Thanksgiving this week in the United States and most governors are admonishing against small gatherings for this traditional family holiday that usually includes large groups that gather together. As I mentioned in the

I Was AFRAID of That!

introduction, this has caused quite the stir in culture and in various camps who believe one way or the other in regard to what should be done and how matters should be handled. Some feel we should shut down the country until there is a vaccine, and others feel there is no need to even wear a mask, social distance or limit social gatherings.

The United States is really divided right now on so many issues and on various fronts. There are still concerns for the economy, unemployment, social injustice, and political corruption. And, on top of all of that, there are the health concerns and death tolls in regards to COVID -19. There is also the pending vaccine and the fear of whether it should even be given, and, if so, should it be taken or not. These issues have created more fear and have caused shortages, and the concern that greater shortages could be seen in the future. For example, I mentioned in the introduction how toilet paper had become a scarcity as people emptied shelves of it to stockpile, and this time it was not only toilet paper, but also paper towels. I guess everyone needed added assurance so they stock piled paper towels as well. All of these concerns and more have seemed to escalate and expose the fear of not having enough.

Chapter 9: Fear of Not Having Enough

And here's the interesting thing about the fear of not having enough: it will cause you to stockpile instead of sharing, hoard instead of giving away, and it will make you stingy instead of being generous. It can also cause you to save fervidly instead of spending wisely. Now the last statement sounds logical and although it is wise to save and it should be practiced, it's not always good for the economy if people become fearful in regard to spending their money on simple commodities and life's true necessities. When you have a fear of not having enough, it may cause you to find comfort in having too much, if you are not careful. I also believe that these practices are opposite of the Kingdom of God and God's principles found in the Bible. The Bible says, *"Give and it will be given to you; pressed down, shaken together and running over."* [xii]

The law of reciprocity is part of the Kingdom of God. And when we have a fear of not having enough, we can actually create the very thing we fear. Let me explain. Reciprocity is *the quality or state of being reciprocal; a mutual dependence, action or influence on the result.* It is mutually corresponding to create a result or outcome that is desired. Therefore, when you have a fear of not having enough, you can block the flow of reciprocity

and in turn create the thing you fear the most: not having enough.

It's amazing how the enemy can discourage us with the fear of not having enough, when we serve a God of more than enough! I believe the fear of not having enough is derived from a spirit of poverty and from the overwhelming sense of lack in our lives that is not always a true reality. If unchecked this will create a stronghold of daily desperation that will affect the way we handle our resources and live our lives. Allow your desperation to drive you to God and allow Him to be your source and satisfaction in all things. Choose to believe the Word! I believe that my God shall supply all of my needs according to his riches in glory.[xiii] I trust the Word of God that declares, *"I've never seen the righteous forsaken or His seed begging for bread."*[xiv] We have to live our lives trusting God and His Word, while resisting the fear of not having enough, because our God is a God of more than enough!

IS MORE THAN ENOUGH REALLY ENOUGH

I remember being offended when I heard a preacher say, *"A mentality that believes as long as I have enough for me and my family, I will be fine, is really a selfish idea to live by."* And, as a side note most new revelations

Chapter 9: Fear of Not Having Enough

that ended up changing my life, offended me at first. Anyway, this was one of those thoughts that introduced a new way of thinking for me in regard to living and giving, and in regard to being set free from the fear of not having enough. You see the reason I was offended at first is because I had a mentality that said, as long as I have just enough, then that is enough. But, let me ask you this: If all I have is just enough for me and my family, then how will I have enough to help or bless someone else? I pray that a light bulb just came on in your thinking and I hope it illuminates the fact that if all you have is only enough for you, at its root, this is a selfish concept and is a narrow-minded marginal way of living.

You will never have more than enough if you are constantly driven by the fear of not having enough. That's because you will eventually run out of what you have by holding on to it. And, if you are controlled by a fear of not having enough, you will never be able to satisfy what you're lacking, by having more. There has to be an inner peace of knowing who your source is, not just in knowing what resources you have. Things can never replace God being your source for all things. Now, let me also interject this: the *fear* of not having enough and *literally* not having enough, are two very different realities. But, in order for you to have peace in the midst of lacking a resource or a need, you must learn to trust God, nonetheless. There may also be times when you have to expand your capacity in order to receive more. And, you may need to start looking at what you do have, and not at what you don't have!

With these thoughts of not having enough, believing for more than enough, trusting God, making God your source, expanding your capacity for more and looking at what you do have instead of at what you don't have, I'm reminded of two Old Testament stories about two widows who had an exchange and an encounter with an Old Testament prophet. One was with the prophet Elisha and one was with the prophet Elijah. One was in regards to some oil and flour and one was in regards to a small jar of olive oil. Both widows had a need and neither had enough to provide for their need or for their future. Here's how the first story unfolds in II Kings chapter four beginning with verse one:

¹ A certain woman of the wives of the sons of the prophets cried out to Elisha, saying, "Your servant my husband is dead, and you know that your servant feared the LORD. And the creditor is coming to take my two sons to be his slaves." ² So Elisha said to her, **"What shall I do for you? Tell me, what do you have in the house?"** *And she said, "Your maidservant has* **nothing in the house** *but a jar of oil." ³ Then he said, "Go,*

Chapter 9: Fear of Not Having Enough

*borrow vessels from everywhere, from all your neighbors— empty vessels; **do not gather just a few**. ⁴And when you have come in, you shall shut the door behind you and your sons; then pour it into all those vessels, and set aside the full ones."*
⁵So she went from him and shut the door behind her and her sons, who brought the vessels to her; and she poured it out.
*⁶**Now it came to pass, when the vessels were full, that she said to her son, "Bring me another vessel." And he said to her, "There is not another vessel." So the oil ceased.** ⁷Then she came and told the man of God. And he said, "Go, sell the oil and pay your debt; and you and your sons live on the rest."*

This story illustrates what I was talking about in regard to looking at what you have instead of looking at what you don't have. And it accentuates the idea that you may have to expand your capacity to receive more. Look at verse two and notice the words that are in bold. The widow asks the prophet for help and he basically says, *"What can I do about it?"* But, he doesn't end the conversation there. He goes on to ask her what she has in her house. In other words, not what don't you have, but rather what do you have. Here's what's interesting! She says, *"I have absolutely nothing! Except for a little jar of oil."* Sometimes you may have to start with what you do have, even if it seems insignificant.

Now here's where the expanding your capacity part comes in. She did as the prophet commanded her and she went and borrowed jars for a surplus of oil. She collected as many as she could find. Before she had anything more than she had started with, she went and

I Was **AFRAID** *of That!*

asked for jars to contain what she was believing for. The widow moved in faith and broke the fear of not having enough! She went back to her house and poured and poured and poured until she had no more jars to pour into. See, I believe if she had had more jars, there would have been more oil. You don't just serve a God of enough, you serve a God of more than enough! Ask Him to expand your capacity for more. He is your source and He can break the fear of not having enough over your life! You can displace your fear by activating your faith. That's what the widows in these stories do. Now let's look at the other story of the widow of Zarephath in I Kings chapter seventeen beginning with verse eight:

[8] Then the word of the LORD came to him, saying, [9] "Arise, go to Zarephath, which belongs to Sidon, and dwell there. See, I have commanded a widow there to provide for you." [10] So he arose and went to Zarephath. And when he came to the gate of the city, indeed a widow was there gathering sticks. And he called to her and said, "Please bring me a little water in a cup, that I may drink." [11] And as she was going to get it, he called to her and said, "Please bring me a morsel of bread in your hand." [12] So she said, **"As the LORD your God lives, I do not have bread, only a handful of flour in a bin, and a little oil in a jar; and see, I am gathering a couple of sticks that I may go in and prepare it for myself and my son, that we may eat it, and die."** *[13] And Elijah said to her,* **"Do not fear;** *go and do as you have said, but* **make me a small cake from it first, and bring it to me; and afterward make some for yourself and your son.** *[14] For thus says the LORD God of Israel: 'The bin of flour shall*

Chapter 9: Fear of Not Having Enough

not be used up, nor shall the jar of oil run dry, until the day the LORD sends rain on the earth." ¹⁵ So she went away and did according to the word of Elijah; and she and he and her household ate for many days. **¹⁶ The bin of flour was not used up, nor did the jar of oil run dry, according to the word of the LORD which He spoke by Elijah.**

Notice the verses that are in bold and what they say in comparison to the fear of not having enough. The widow says, *"I swear by God that all I have is a little flour and a little oil and I'm going to take it and make a pancake for me and my son and then we will eat and die because there will be no more left."* Talk about a situation. Talk about a dilemma. Talk about a scenario. Nevertheless, look at what the prophet tells her in verse thirteen: **"DO NOT FEAR!"** But wait a minute. The prophet then tells her to make a pancake for him and bring it to him, before she makes one for herself and for her son.

Can you imagine the faith it took to make a pancake and take to the prophet first, not knowing for certain that there would be enough left for her and her son if she did obey his command? Here's what happened: Faith collided with the fear of not having enough, and faith won! She gave what she had and received more than she began with. Wow! Look at verse sixteen, *"The bin of flour was not used up, nor did the jar of oil run dry."* She had a momentary problem that was turned into an eternal provision, all because she was obedient and gave what was not enough away anyway, and in return received more than enough!

More than enough is always enough when God is in it! Let me illustrate with another biblical story about a little lad who goes unnamed, but seems to be the only one out of thousands of people that has anything to eat at lunchtime. He gave his lunch away before he could eat lunch. Sounds familiar doesn't it? Whenever there is lack in the Bible, it seems faith and giving are always the solution to the problem. That's also because any fear, including the fear of not having enough, has to be conquered through faith!

Faith is trusting God to be who He said He is, and it is believing that He will do what He said He would do, even when it seems impossible. There was one young boy with a small lunch and Jesus took it, broke it and blessed it. Then He gave it away and fed over five thousand people, including the little lad with the lunch that started it all. Did I mention there were twelve baskets full leftover? Again, it's amazing how the enemy can discourage us with the fear of not having enough, when we serve a God of more than enough!

Chapter 10

Fear of Missing It

Areas Where You May Have a Fear of Missing It:
- Missing an Opportunity to Do Good
- Missing God's Will for Your Life
- Missing an Investment Opportunity
- Missing a Deadline at Work or School
- Missing a Special Moment in Time or in Life

WHAT DOES MISSING IT REALLY MEAN

What do I mean by missing it? First of all, I mean an opportunity that has passed you by, and secondly, I mean an impression, chance, idea or occasion that you didn't see, seize or sense until it was too late. Now let's look at these words individually and then we will look at them again in context as we continue this chapter. The definition for the word *"missing"* of course is fairly obvious. It would mean something that no longer exists or that doesn't appear obvious or obtainable anymore. The word "*It,*" however, could mean several things, but, in this case, "It" would primarily deal with

I Was **AFRAID** *of That!*

an opportunity that seems to no longer exist to be seized, enjoyed or experienced.

The fear of *missing it* is a feeling that you messed up by missing out on an opportunity that was just for you. We looked at the words "*missing*" and "*it*," but remember the word *fear* is defined as *a strong unpleasant emotion*. So, when you put the statement "Fear of Missing It" together, it would mean: *A strong unpleasant emotion caused by an awareness that an opportunity that once existed, now appears to be unobtainable or maybe even non-existent*. This is what I mean when I'm talking about the *fear of missing it*. In other words, it is a feeling of regret because a desired opportunity that could have been seized, no longer exists because of a choice that you did or didn't make.

The fear of missing it encompasses all facets of time including past, present and future. In regard to the past, it would be the fear that you missed a moment or opportunity that has already happened because you weren't sure that it was right or best at the time. Concerning the present, it would be the fear of missing a 'now' moment if it is not acted upon because you are not certain of the outcome or you don't have the courage to act because the ultimate result is unknown.

Chapter 10: Fear of Missing It

And lastly, in regard to the future, it would be the fear of missing an event or opportunity that is going to happen in the future because you weren't aware of it or you didn't feel like you had adequate time to process or prepare with the information you needed to make a healthy judgment or decision.

Fear itself invites you to believe in something and the fear of "missing it" invites you to believe that you only had one choice or one opportunity, and that's not always the case. I believe we serve a God of second chances and I believe if you missed it, He will give you another opportunity that may even be better than what you previously felt that you missed out on. As a matter of fact, missing an opportunity could lead to a lesson learned or a greater opportunity experienced. Nonetheless, I want you to know this: The battle is always in the mind! That's why you have to renew your mind with the Word of God and fight against what discourages you and tries to defeat you. Here are some areas that you may have to fight against if you feel like you have missed it:

- Regret
- Discouragement
- Second-guessing Yourself
- Comparing

- Anger
- Frustration
- Despair

The fear of missing it is a delusional enemy that will keep you bound to an analysis paralysis scenario that will ultimately produce discouragement while robbing you of your peace and stealing your joy. Don't allow the regret of yesterday or the fear of tomorrow to steal the peace of mind that you deserve today! Fear is a thief. It is an emotional demoralizer that triggers distress and creates despair. The fear of missing it will cause you to second guess yourself. It will create a stronghold of debilitating discouragement that left undealt with could lead to an even greater despair. If you don't shift your focus, despair will lead to defeat and you will be forfeiting your joy and peace over what you can't do anything about now.

Discouragement will turn to despair and it will keep you from having peace over the past and it will also keep you from having hope for the future. And worst of all, if you constantly live with the fear of *missing it*- you will ultimately miss it! If you are always fixated with the thought that you missed an opportunity, or a God moment, or even a moment in time, you will miss your present opportunities, all because you have chosen to

Chapter 10: Fear of Missing It

focus on what no longer exists. Don't allow the fear of missing it to cause you to miss out on what is right in front of you at this very moment.

Here's the thing, you will miss "it" again if you don't learn to focus on what is in front of you and stop focusing on what is behind you. The fear of "missing it" many times is a fear over something that has already happened or has passed you by. For the most part it is an unpleasant emotion that is being experienced because of something that has already happened. You fear that you have "missed it." However, I also realize that you can fear missing out on something in the future as well. The reason that I mention this is because most of the fears that we have dealt with so far and that we will deal with in the remainder of this book, deal with either the fear of a present situation or the fear of a future outcome, not fear over something that has already taken place.

The fear of "missing it" primarily deals with an opportunity, moment or situation that has already happened. I don't want to see the fear of missing it keep you bound to the past. In Philippians 3:13, Paul tells us to forget the past and reach for the future! The word forget is not saying you forget by accident, but rather you forget on purpose. You have to forget on purpose by not rehearsing the regret! Don't fear what you have missed, be thankful for what you have right now. Don't look back in regret and despair, look to the future with hope and expectation. Don't keep rehearsing dismal scenarios over and over again. Know and believe that all things work together for good. Learn the lesson and don't repeat the pattern. Ask God for another opportunity. Displace the fear of missing it at the core of your life by believing that God is a God of second chances. You can also find peace in the realization that maybe what you missed wasn't for you, and, if it was, God will bring it back around again, in His time.

CAN YOU REALLY MISS IT

The fear of missing it also has, at the heart of it, a sense that what you have chosen is not best or as beneficial as something else may have been or could have been. It carries with it the thought of missing out on what might have been and it also creates the feeling that you will miss out on what is next or best. It can produce a sense of regret that, left undealt with will create a discouragement that will cause you to second guess yourself. But I want you to know that you are sufficient in Him! I believe that you have everything that you

Chapter 10: Fear of Missing It

need to seize any moment that God sets before you, at any given moment. I declare over you that you have discretion, discernment, wisdom, courage and good judgement! And I believe that as long as you are walking in obedience and being sensitive to the Holy Spirit's promptings, it will be hard for you to miss what God has for you. If you don't have your eyes closed, your fingers in your ears and your heart closed off to the things around you, then you won't miss what God has for you to experience or obtain.

I chose this chapter on the fear of *missing it* because after being in full-time vocational ministry for thirty-seven years, I've had numerous people ask me, "How do I know if I did or didn't miss it?" "And, what do I do now, if I did miss it?" In most of these cases, if not all of them, I believe these people were referring to a prompting from God to be obedient to an opportunity that, at the time, seemed divine. And, for the countless others that didn't express concern in verbal terms, I believe many still wondered the same: "Did I miss it?" You may be grappling with this same question: "Did I miss it and what do I do now?" Here's what I believe after all of these years: God is a good God! He is a good Father. And the Word of God tells us that if earthly fathers know how to give good gifts, then how much more will your heavenly Father give good gifts to those who ask? So what I'm saying is, "Ask!" Ask God for another opportunity and then ask Him for a peace over the opportunity that was lost- the opportunity that you can't do anything about now. And, believe Him for another chance, or believe Him for a peace that passes all understanding so you can get over what you can't change or don't understand.

A peace that passes all understanding is a beautiful thing because there are so many things we won't be able to understand or that we can't change. We need God's peace to surpass those things that we can't understand and that we can't change, so that we can have peace in our lives. Because what the fear of *missing it* will do is, it will keep you tied to doubting and second guessing and it will keep you from trying something new or different. Nevertheless, I want you to know that I believe that your faith is not so fragile that if you do get off track or you actually do miss it for the moment, that God through His faithful eternal GPS, can get you back on track by His grace and through His love. There is no reason to allow the fear of missing it to cause you to despair, when you serve a God of second chances.

Chapter 11

Fear of the Unknown

*Faith is the substance of things hoped
for, the evidence of things not seen.*
- Hebrews 11:1

DON'T LET THAT STOP YOU

You will never fully know everyone or everything, but don't let that stop you from living life. Faith is about trusting what you can't see and every step of faith begins with the unknown. Moses didn't know that the Red Sea would part until he stretched out his rod in faith over the water. Noah didn't know it would rain until he built the ark. Shadrach, Meshach and Abednego didn't know they would survive the fiery furnace until they walked through the fire and the Lord walked with them. Abraham didn't know God would provide a lamb until he laid Isaac on the altar. David didn't know the giant would fall until he released the stone from his slingshot. Paul didn't know the prison doors would open until he and Silas began to pray and sing. The woman with the issue of blood didn't know she would be made whole until she touched the hem of

Jesus' garment. Peter didn't know Jesus would reach down and lift him up out of the water until he stepped out the boat and began to sink. The little lad with the lunch didn't know if he would eat after he gave his lunch away, but he was part of a huge miracle that day when over five thousand people were fed with just his lunch. The unknown will always be unknown to us, but not to God, because He sees and knows everything.

Obedience is the crucible that produced the outcome that was believed for in every one of these biblical scenarios that you just read about in the previous paragraph. If you are going to see a desirable result from a seemingly insurmountable situation that has an unknown outcome, you will be required to move in faith, not knowing what the result might be. Faith is about being obedient and obedience many times unlocks the unknown, but it will take courage to step out in faith to see it revealed. Remember, courage doesn't mean you don't have fear, it means you have the audacity to act in spite of your fear or in spite of how you may feel at the time. You may have to face your fear and move in faith by being obedient through courage in order to receive the outcome you truly desire. God knows and He sees! And He will be faithful towards you just like He was toward the people in

Chapter 11: Fear of the Unknown

these biblical accounts in the section above. You may not see or know, but God does. You may not know what lies on the other side of the unknown, but God does! Being obedient to what you know is right is your responsibility; the outcome is God's responsibility!

However, with all of that being said, I want you to know that obedience is never easy. That's because the ultimate outcome is not revealed until you act upon what is being required of you to do by faith before you see or know the outcome. The result is usually not revealed until you respond by being obedient through faith. And, faith will usually look foolish until the outcome you are believing for is manifested or seen. But know this: faith and obedience will always be the precursors to breaking any fear that has control over your life, especially the fear of the unknown. Obedience will also be necessary for you to see, by faith, the outcome that you truly desire to see and know. Even so, it will still take courage to face what you fear and it will take courage to act in obedience despite how you may be feeling about the unknown situation that you are facing. The unknown will always be unknown on this side of what you can't see or don't know. It takes faith to believe without seeing, and it takes courage to respond in spite of being afraid.

I don't want to see you be so hindered by fear that it keeps you from experiencing all that God has for you. I don't want you to be so gripped by fear that you never know the joy of surrendering to what seems to be blind obedience. I don't want to see you live another day with fear robbing you of your joy and peace all because what you are facing is unknown. I believe in the midst of the unknown that a determined obedience will produce divine results. Obedience and faith are the only way to combat a fear of the unknown. Hebrews 11:1 says *"Faith is the substance of things hoped for the evidence of things not seen."* Even when you can't see, you still have to believe and put your trust in a God who sees and knows all things.

DO IT ANYWAY

Don't let what you can't control, control you! You can't control what is unknown or uncertain. You can't control the future. A fear of the future and the fear of the unknown are very similar in the fact that they both deal with something that lies ahead that is unsure, uncertain or unknown. I want you to know that you can trust an unknown future to a known and proven God. He is with you and He is more than enough! Don't allow a stronghold of skeptical speculation be created because you fear the unknown more than you trust

Chapter 11: Fear of the Unknown

God. Skeptical speculation would be defined as doubtful assumption. In other words, it would mean that you have developed a mindset that assumes and doubts a reality that you can experience, all because you are being faced with a scenario that is uncertain or unknown.

> *The oldest and strongest emotion of mankind is fear, and the oldest and strongest kind of fear is fear of the unknown.*
> – H.P. Lovecraft

> *We do not fear the unknown. We fear what we think we know about the unknown.*
> – Teal Swan

> *Fear not the unknown. It is a sea of possibilities.*
> – Tom Althouse

There will never be a time when everything you desire to know will be known. You can plan and you can prepare, but there is nothing for certain except for God and everything that His word possesses and promises. You can vote, but you alone can't control who the next president is going to be or know the result before the process is completed. You can stockpile and hoard food and toilet paper and paper towels, but you alone can't control the ebb and flow of the supply and demand curve or know if there will be enough of what you desire when you need it. You can wear a mask, social distance, self-quarantine and wash your hands more frequently, but you alone can't control when or if the COVID 19 pandemic will end allowing you to resume societal activities that you are accustomed to.

There are so many variables in life that are unknown, uncertain and uncontrollable. You have to live, learn, grow and risk in spite of not knowing the outcome of every experience. The only way to truly conquer the fear of the unknown is to do it anyway! You have to be wise, be discerning, be cautious and be prepared. But, there is no way to know the exact outcome of every occasion, scenario, experience or venture. However, the word of God reminds us that the Lord orders our steps and the word of God tells us that He establishes our end from our beginning and our beginning from our end. God is faithful and He can't be anything other than who He is. You can trust an unknown future to a known and proven God. Remember, don't let what you can't control, control you! You have to live by faith and trust God with the outcome, even if the outcome is unknown. You can trust God because the unknown is not unknown to Him!

Chapter 12

Fear of Others' Opinions

Opinion [əˈpinyən] – 1. a view, judgment or appraisal formed in the mind about something, not necessarily based on fact or knowledge. 2. the beliefs or views of a large number or majority of people about a particular thing. 3. an estimation of the quality or worth of someone or something.

JUDGEMENT, PERSUASION AND VALUE

Someone will always have an opinion about something or someone and the target of that opinion might just be you. So, some questions for you may then be, *"Whose opinion matters and whose opinion do you value?"* You should also consider why their opinion matters or bothers you? Not all opinions are right and not all opinions should be voiced. That's because an opinion brings with it a sense of judgement. It also carries with it a weight of persuasion. What others say or think about you may even affect the way you see yourself and it could determine the way you feel about others as well. Opinions that you value or that persuade you actually function as crucibles that, in turn, form your perspective. The reason that this is important to realize is because the lens through which you see things, determines what you see. Therefore, an opinion can persuade how you see things.

I realize I could have entitled this chapter: Fear of What Others' May Think or Fear of What Others' Say About You. Because in reality, that's what an opinion is. It's what someone would think or say about you. But the reality of the matter is, it doesn't matter what you do or don't do, someone will have an opinion about it. But you can't allow the negative opinions of others to affect you in a negative way. If you don't learn to deal with the fear of others' opinions, it will create a stronghold of guarded gestures. What I mean by that is this: it will affect the way that you say things, do things and react to things. It will stifle the way that you share your feelings and express yourself. It will also impact how you deal with others.

Left undealt with, the fear of others' opinions will create insecurities and cause you to develop a sense of inferiority. Don't allow it to! Eleanor Roosevelt says, *"No one can make you feel inferior without your consent."* I want you to know that you are not inferior. You are not mediocre! You are wonderfully and fearfully made in the image of God. You are the

Chapter 12: Fear of Others' Opinions

workmanship of His hands. You are uniquely and gloriously created by a creative and loving God. You are unique and you have value, worth, purpose and meaning. I bet you can see by now that the fear of not being good enough and the fear of others' opinions are closely linked in comparison much like the fear of the future and the fear of the unknown. That's because the fear of not being good enough and the fear of others' opinions both deal with the issue of acceptance.

But, nonetheless, just like in the chapter on the fear of not being good enough, I want you to know that you are enough and that you are made in the image of God. And, although others will form and express their opinions about you, it's what God and His word say about you that matters the most! All opinions are not true; they are just an opinion. But, what God says about you through His word is truth, not an opinion. Don't allow the opinions of others to determine what you do or don't do. You've already been accepted and you have already been approved by God.

The fear of others' opinions about you primarily deals with acceptance and approval. It deals with concerns such as these: *"Is who I am good enough?"* Or, *"Is what I did worthy enough to be approved or accepted by*

I Was AFRAID of That!

anyone?" Here's one thing that may help you fight against the fear of others' opinions, and that is to remember this: it's just someone's opinion! And like they say, "Everyone has one!" In other words, at any given moment anyone can form or give an opinion about you or what you have done. And, social media has escalated people's opinions!

Everyone feels that they have a voice and that they can share their opinions anytime they choose on whatever matter they deem worthy, including you and your family. People voice opinions, take sides and form allegiances. This can vary from personal to political and these differences of opinions can create frustration, confusion, doubt and uncertainty. There are two different sides to every story and there are usually two different opinions in regard to the why or the why not's and the should and the should not's of any scenario.

Now more than ever in the midst of the COVID 19 pandemic and just after the recent presidential election, people have varying opinions. There are so many issues that are being made political, besides the presidential election. Some of these include the issue of should you wear a mask or not? Should businesses remain open for business or shut down until the

Chapter 12: Fear of Others' Opinions

pandemic is over or at least in decline? Who should be president and who should not? Was the election fair or was there voter fraud that swayed the election one way or another? Should the police be supported or defunded? Should schools remain open or close down? Should we go back to "things as usual" or should there be a "new normal"?

And then you add these opinions to the conspiracy theories, which in turn create more anxiety and uncertainty, putting stress and fear at an all-time high. Nonetheless, whether it is personal or political, people will always have an opinion. And these opinions can take a toll on your mental well-being. However, this chapter is not just about opinions, it's about the fear of others' opinions in regard to what they might say or think about you. It's about you not allowing the fear of what others may say about you affect you in a negative way. Don't allow others' opinions to hinder you or hold you back in any way, shape or form. Don't allow people's opinion to persuade you into believing their overbearing opinion over a realistic reality. You can't allow the fear of others' opinions to keep you from reaching your full potential. Don't allow what others say stop you from obtaining all that God has for you.

APPLAUSE, CRITICISM AND CONFIRMATION

Dr. Henry Cloud, author of the popular book, Boundaries, says that we should weigh critics, not count them. Did you get that? It's not about how many critics you have, it's about how many of those opinions matter to you. It's not about how many opinions you hear, it's about the weight that they carry and how you allow them to impact you and your decisions. Don't allow what you can't control, control you! You have more going for you than you do that is against you. Remember, if you feel like that you have messed up and people are giving their negative opinion about what you did, a momentary setback is not a lifetime sentence and their opinion is just that: it's an opinion. What God and His Word says about you is all that truly matters. God calls you blessed, healed, hopeful and forgiven. Don't allow the fear of others' opinions to offend you or keep you from a blessed life and a hopeful future. In a world full of opinions, the only opinions that truly matters are the one's that you form for yourself that is based upon God's love and grace, and is reflected and seen in His word.

In chapter 5, we dealt the fear of rejection and I talked about Jesus being baptized and the Holy Spirit ascending upon Him like a dove and the heavens

Chapter 12: Fear of Others' Opinions

opening and the Lord declaring, *"This is my Son in whom I'm well pleased."* In chapter 5 I also mentioned how Jesus had the approval of God, not by merit or by earning it, but because He was His Son. It's amazing when God or the Bible recognizes something as being right or good, Satan or somebody attacks it. That's what opinions sometimes do, they attack something that is valid, authentic, wholesome or true. People do this by using words that create a conflict or cast a shadow of doubt on what's being said or done. In the gospel of Matthew, the story is recorded of Jesus' baptism and His being led into the wilderness to be tempted by Satan. It shows Jesus' identity being announced and attacked one right after the other. In Matthew chapter 3 the heavens open and the Lord declares, *"This is my Son in whom I'm well pleased"* and then in the very next chapter Satan says, *"If you are the Son of God..."*

Look at Matthew 3:16-17 and Matthew 4:1-3:

Matthew 3:16-17: *¹⁶When He had been baptized, Jesus came up immediately from the water; and behold, the heavens were opened to Him, and He saw the Spirit of God descending like a dove and lighting upon Him. ¹⁷And suddenly a voice came from heaven, saying,* **"This is My Beloved Son,** *in whom I am well pleased."*

I Was **AFRAID** *of That!*

Matthew 4:1-3: ¹*Then Jesus was led up by the Spirit into the wilderness to be tempted by the devil.* ²*And when He had fasted forty days and forty nights, afterward He was hungry.* ³*Now when the tempter came to Him, he said,* **"If You are the Son of God,** *command that these stones become bread."*

Notice that Satan attacks what God said. He casts a shadow of doubt by asking a question and by demanding the truth, but the truth has already been established. Sound familiar? That's right! In the garden with Adam and Eve, He did the same thing. Nonetheless, he says to Jesus, *"If You are the Son of God."* Wait a minute! God is the one that declared Jesus was the Son of God. Not Jesus Himself, but God. Satan must have been listening and Matthew records the scenario in back to back verses in back to back chapters of his gospel. Here's my point, our identity has to be found in Christ and in Christ alone. Not my opinion, not your opinion, but in the truth of what God's word declares and establishes. What Satan said was an accusation that threatened the identity of Christ and questioned the truth that good had already declared.

Don't allow people's opinion of you or something that you believe in to do the same thing. Don't allow those opinions to make you doubt or cower in fear. Jesus constantly had people saying who they thought He

Chapter 12: Fear of Others' Opinions

was. He continually had those who gave their demands and opinions about what He had done or about what they thought He should do. Jesus once had a dialogue with His disciples and He asked them. *"Who do you say I am?"* In other words, everyone else has their opinion of who they say I am, so who do you say I am. It's interesting because in this same dialogue Peter answers, *"You are the Son of the living God."* To which Jesus replies, *"You have answered correctly, but flesh and blood has not revealed this to you, but it was my Father in heaven that has revealed this to you."* One translation says, *"It was not a human being that revealed this to you, but it was my Father in Heaven that revealed it to you."* What if our revelation came from our heavenly Father and not human beings? I believe that we would have a greater understanding of what we value and why.

I also believe that the fear of others' opinions wouldn't affect us in a negative way if we found our true sense of being and our rightful identity in the One who made us, loves us and empowers us to live and move and have our being in Him. You can't live by someone's criticism or compliments. You can't live or die by the opinions that someone forms about you. It is vital for you to not live with a fear of others' opinions. Base

your decisions and security on who you are in Christ and what God's word says you are and on what it says you have.

The fear of others opinions will cause you to either not do anything because you are afraid of what others might say, or it will cause you to do things in order to receive applause and acceptance from others based upon what you do or don't do. Neither is healthy. When you allow the opinions of others to become self-reflected in a way that is negative, it can cause debilitating behaviors. I don't want to see this be the case with you. After coming off of a 40 day fast a few years ago, I feel like I was delivered from the fear of what others thought, and it was liberating!

I realized that no matter what I did, someone would form an opinion about it. Therefore, I refocused on the Lord, myself and those whose opinions mattered the most to me. It is my prayer that you will be set free from the fear of the opinions of others. I pray that you will be liberated from what others think. It is my desire that you will realize there is a difference between fact and opinion. God's word is fact; man's opinions are just that: opinions. Don't allow what someone else may say or think about you hinder you any longer!

SECTION III
ASSUMPTIONS AND ANTIDOTES

Chapter 13

Illusions and Realities

- **Illusion** [iˈlo͞oZHən] - *a thing that is or is likely to be wrongly perceived or interpreted by the senses.*
    1. a deceptive appearance or impression.
    2. a false idea or belief.
    3. misleading image presented to the vision.
    4. something that deceives or misleads.
    5. a perception existing in such a way as to cause misinterpretation of its actual being or nature.

- **Reality** [rēˈalədē] - *the world or the state of things as they actually exist, as opposed to an idealistic or notional idea of them.*
    - a thing that is actually experienced or seen.
    - a thing that exists in fact.
    - the state or quality of having existence or substance.

SHADOWS, SENSES AND SOUNDS

Have you ever been awakened in the night and thought that someone was in the room? Only to turn on a light and realize that it was just your clothes that you threw over a chair or the treadmill. Or, how about being awakened in the night to the sound of something that startled you so bad that it made you think that someone was in the house, but instead it was just the

HVAC unit turning on or off. It's amazing how sounds, shadows, reflections and strange noises can stimulate fear at the most vulnerable and unplanned times. What we fear is not always a reality. Many have used the acronym F.E.A.R. in regard to the word fear. The letters in the acronym stand for: **F**alse **E**vidence **A**ppearing **R**eal. It is evidence that appears real but is not apparent in reality. It would be something fabricated in one's mind or stimulated by an external noise, shadow or movement that seemed real, but in fact, was not in reality harmful or dangerous.

When there is false evidence appearing real, this means there is no true threat of physical danger, no threat of the loss of someone or something that is dear to you. There is nothing there at all but **F.E.A.R.**, a false evidence appearing real. A reality and an illusion are two different things. Reality is an actual fact. An illusion is a misleading image that deceives someone intellectually. But, an illusion can be so strong it may seem real. Fear will activate your emotions and stimulate your senses while creating an illusion of a false reality. An illusion is a phenomenon involving your perception of reality. Illusions are perceived and distorted. A reality is actual and factual. Many fears that we experience exist in our minds more than they

Chapter 13: Illusions and Realities

do in actual reality. You can talk yourself into being afraid by escalating what is going on around you by exaggerating it in your mind. Your mind and emotions can take over if you let them! Don't be controlled by what you can't control and don't fear what doesn't need to be feared.

Nonetheless, what I'm trying to say is this: fear will sometimes make an illusion appear as a reality. Sometimes there's an escalated exaggerated feeling more than there is an actual reality of danger or harm. In the Bible there are many scenarios where assumptions become perception because fear exaggerated reality. Think about the disciples in the middle of a storm fearing for their lives when Jesus appears to them walking on the water. They were so afraid that they thought that He was a ghost. Their assumption created a perception and their perception created an illusion and their illusion created a false reality. And all of this happened all because of fear. And, all of their thoughts were fabricated and transcribed in their minds first. They saw through the eyes of fear an illusion that in turn created a reality that didn't actually exist. But, thank God every time we experience fear, just like the disciples on the sea, Jesus is there saying, *"Fear not! I am with you."* I thank God that we can have this confidence that He will never leave us or forsake us, especially when we fear.

Most fears are an illusion that is created in your own mind. Someone said 90% of the things that we worry about never come to pass. I would say the same about fear. I would say that 90% of the things we fear never come to pass or never actually exist in reality. I would also say this: don't allow your mind to create scenarios that will cause you to fear things that in reality might not even happen. Your mind has the power to minimize or maximize what you see, hear and believe. I don't want to see you limited by a fear that has been created in your mind, but that actually doesn't exist, or at least it doesn't exist in reality to the magnitude that it does in your mind. I don't want you to allow fear to minimize your life's experiences. [xv]Dr. Henry Cloud says, *"Every time that you listen to fear, your world gets smaller."* I don't want to see this happen to you! I don't want to see your world get smaller, I want to see it get bigger and bigger. I want to see hope arise and hopelessness dissipate. I don't want to see fear dictate what you do or don't do. I want to see peace and possibilities become the reality of your life both now and in the future.

Chapter 13: Illusions and Realities

ILLUSIONS, ASSUMPTIONS AND SELF-DOUBT

Fear is an illusion that can distort reality. It can keep you from knowing, seeing or experiencing what's on the other side of what you fear the most. Most fears are bigger in your head and heart than they are in reality. Don't allow an illusion-produced fear dictate what you do or don't do. Although an illusion is not a reality, it can become a reality in your mind. I saw this reality vs. illusion scenario depicted in a Spiderman movie. In the movie the enemy of Spiderman, *Mysterio* used deception and delusion to create an alternative reality to try and defeat Spiderman. *Mysterio* created an illusion with drones to create fear and to develop things that he could destroy, so that he could conquer the illusion and become the hero of the story. *Mysterio* used the illusion-generating capabilities of the drones to create advanced holographic projections, making Peter Parker, a shy, nerdy high school student whose alter ego is Spiderman, believe that he was meeting with Nick Fury and Maria Hill. However, Spiderman knew that if he could get beyond the illusion that Mysterio had created, he could destroy the reality it was creating while stopping the destruction it was causing. That's what you have to do in regard to fear and the illusions that it has created. You have to get

I Was **AFRAID** *of That!*

beyond what you believe in your head and in your heart. You have to get to the bottom of what is really going on so that you don't let it defeat you. You have to move beyond what someone else has told you. You have to stand against the lies of your enemy, Satan and believe the truth of God's word. There are always three enemies at work in your life: yourself, others and Satan. Don't allow any of these to create an illusion-based reality that causes you to respond in fear.

Don't allow an illusion-based reality to cause you to cower in fear. An illusion-based reality would be a reality that you or someone else has created in theory, but in reality it is non-existent. These illusions that distort reality and arouse fear usually begin with assumptions, perceptions and self-doubt. Remember this, everything begins somewhere and nothing exists without an origin. That's why it's important for us to take every thought captive that exalts itself against the knowledge and love of God. You have the authority in Christ and you have the power through the Holy Spirit to control your mind. I have experienced first-hand fearing something that in reality didn't exist. I have feared not being liked or not being accepted, which in reality wasn't the case. I have feared not succeeding, but yet I succeeded. I have feared the darkness of night

Chapter 13: Illusions and Realities

only to find out there was nothing to fear but darkness. I have feared being wrong, but I was actually right. I have feared being misunderstood only to find out that what I was conveying was crystal clear. And, if you remember the note from the author at the beginning of this book, you will remember that I feared riding a roller coaster that in retrospect didn't cause me harm or kill me. Actually it was rather enjoyable once I got past my initial fear and enjoyed the ride while screaming my head off.

I want to see you face your fear and enjoy life. I want to see you sift through the smokescreens that fear has caused you to believe. I want to see you prove to yourself and everyone else for that matter, that fear is sometimes an illusion that just needs to be faced and figured out. And, just like Spiderman you will come to realize that once the illusion is exposed and you face what you fear, there will be power and clarity on the other side of the facade that was being created. I want you to be able to stand against fear and sift through the assumptions, perceptions and self-doubt that are creating the illusion and causing the fear. When it comes to **assumptions** *(what you assume to be true)*, **perceptions** *(a mental image or concept or a physical sensation being created)* and **self-doubt** *(uncertainty*

I Was **AFRAID** *of That!*

about one's abilities or actions) I'm always reminded of the story of the Philippian jailer in Acts 16. Paul and Silas were imprisoned and they prayed and sang praises to God at midnight. As they sang, there was an earthquake and the prison was shaken and all of the doors of the prison were opened and the prisoners' chains were loosed. So, when the Philippian jailer was awakened to the situation, he drew his sword and was about to kill himself, supposing that the prisoners had fled. There's the key word, he supposed or he assumed! He feared the worst before he had a real reason to do so. But, Paul cried out with a loud voice saying, *"Do yourself no harm for we are all here."* The prison guard called for a light and fell down in fear before Paul and Silas and he asked them how to be saved. Sometimes the only way to stand against delusional fear is to speak up and speak out in truth and love. The only way to defeat fear and darkness is to shine a light and let reality be revealed. Don't assume the worst, assume the best. Don't allow perception to dictate reality and don't doubt who you are in Christ! Doubt your doubts and face your fears and watch your future unfold in ways you can't imagine.

Chapter 14

Fear vs. Faith

Faith [fāTH] NOUN
1. complete trust or confidence in someone or something.
   synonyms: trust · belief · confidence · hope · expectation
2. strong belief in God or in the doctrines of biblical principles.

Fear [ˈfir]
NOUN
1. an unpleasant emotion caused by the belief that someone or something is dangerous, likely to cause pain, or a threat.
   synonyms: terror · fright · horror · alarm · panic · agitation

VERB
1. be afraid of (someone or something) as likely to be dangerous, painful, or threatening.
   synonyms: be scared of · be apprehensive of · dread

FEAR AND FAITH BOTH PRODUCE RESULTS

Fear can cause you to worry about something that may never happen. It can cause you to imagine the worst and exaggerate the obvious. Fear can affect your life in so many different ways. It can affect you mentally, physically, relationally and spiritually. Fear can make your knees wobble. It can make your feet slip or stumble. Fear can make your voice tremble. It can make your voice change in pitch or volume. It can make you irrational and insecure. It can make you doubt what you know or question what you are seeing. Fear is an emotion that left uncontrolled will control you in ways that you couldn't imagine. Fear can cause you to lose control of bodily functions and rational behaviors. It will create facades and produce anger. It will make you scream, laugh or cry involuntarily. It is an emotion that left unchallenged will affect you in so many ways. Fear produces results. It will cause you to do what you didn't think you would do and it will cause you to react in ways that you never thought you would react.

Faith, however, is the substance of things hoped for, the evidence of things not seen. Faith will cause you to believe and to trust when you don't have a reason to. It will cause you to hope for the best when the worst seems inevitable. Faith will give you peace in the midst of turmoil. It will give you courage in the midst of wanting to cower and give up. Faith will make you keep going when you want to give up. It will make you calm in the midst of chaos. Faith will be a light in darkness and a calm assurance in the face of the unknown. Faith will make you stand on nothing and believe for the impossible. It will enlighten you. It will empower you to overcome. It will help you see what you couldn't otherwise see. Faith will allow you to know what you

Chapter 14: Fear vs. Faith

didn't know and it will empower you to be more than you thought you could ever be. Faith will save you and keep you. Faith will give you a new found perspective. It will assure you of a relationship with God and give you the assurance of an eternity with Him. Faith is a repairer. It is a restorer! Faith is a redemptive grace that will heal you by helping you to overcome fear while empowering you to walk in freedom.

SEE, SAY, DO, THINK AND BELIEVE

Fear and faith will both produce results and they will both cause you to see, say, do, think and believe what you otherwise wouldn't. Here are some similar ways that fear and faith may cause you to respond:

>**Fear Will Make You:**

1. See What You Normally Wouldn't See. Fear will make you see a person where there's a shadow. It will make you see trouble where there is no danger. One of the first questions you will ask when you are afraid is: *"Did you hear that?"* And usually the second question will be: *"Did you see that?"* Fear will make you see what you normally wouldn't see.

>**Faith Will Make You:**

1. See What You Normally Wouldn't See. Faith will allow you to see things before they are tangible. It will create an opportunity for you to see things as God does. Faith will align itself with the Word of God, not

the world around you. It will allow you to see your position in Christ, not your literal condition in this world. In other words, you may feel like you're going through hell, but the Bible tells you that you are seated in heavenly places with Christ. Faith looks foolish until the promise you're believing for is manifested. Faith comes by hearing and believing, not by seeing, but, it will affect how you see things. Abraham had faith and it was accounted to him as righteousness. He had to believe the promise of God for a child in his old age with a wife who was beyond childbearing age. He had to look beyond His wife's womb to receive the word of the Lord. Faith will make you see what you don't see in the natural world. *I see myself saved, healed and whole!* I see myself complete and lacking nothing. Faith will make you see what you normally wouldn't see.

>**Fear Will Make You:**

2. Say What You Wouldn't Normally Say. Fear will make you scream. It will cause you to stutter and stammer. Fear will make you lash out in anger. It could cause you to *curse*. Fear will make you say things that you will regret. Fear will cause you to make promises you can't keep. Fear will make you say what you might not normally say.

>**Faith Will Make You:**

2. Say What You Wouldn't Normally Say. Just like fear can make you look foolish, faith sometimes can, too. The reason faith will appear foolish is because you are

Chapter 14: Fear vs. Faith

talking about what you can't see. You are speaking by faith and faith is the substance of things hoped for, the evidence of things not seen. So when I am facing something I can't handle on my own, I say, *"I can do all things through Christ who gives me strength."* And when I do, I'm speaking in faith. When I am facing something that seems unconquerable, I say, *"I am an overcomer through Christ Jesus who loved me and gave Himself for me."* Faith allows me to say something that I usually wouldn't say. I'm speaking words of faith, even when I can't see it in the natural. Faith will make you say what you normally wouldn't say!

>**Fear Will Make You:**

3. Do What You Wouldn't Normally Do. Fear will make you run. It will cause to trip and fall. It will make you hit someone. Fear will make you cry. It could cause you to faint. Fear can make you wet yourself or soil your undergarments. It can make you short of breath, causing you to gasp for air. Fear will make you do what you would not do under normal circumstances.

>**Faith Will Make You:**

3. Do What You Wouldn't Normally Do. Faith will cause you to love the unlovable when you don't really want to. It will allow you to love when you deep down want to hate or resent. Faith will allow you to forgive because you know that you've been forgiven by grace through faith. And faith allows you to know that true forgiveness comes by not only being forgiven, but by

also forgiving. It will make you pray when you don't feel like it. Faith will cause you to give when you want to keep something or to hold back. It will give you the courage to believe when you don't have a reason to believe. Faith will make you do what you wouldn't normally do.

>**Fear Will Make You:**

4. Think What You Wouldn't Normally Think. Fear will make you think (assume) what you normally wouldn't think. It will make you think that someone is out to get you. Fear can make you think that someone is following you. It will make you think that you are in danger when in actuality you are safe and not really in danger of being harmed. Thinking occurs in the mind and deepens with one's imagination. Fear than, only exaggerates whatever is transpiring. Therefore, what you're thinking can escalate quickly when you are afraid. You can think there's someone outside trying to get in the house and it can escalate to thinking that they're in the house and going to harm you. Fear will make you think what you normally wouldn't think.

>**Faith Will Make You:**

4. Think What You Wouldn't Normally Think. Faith will make you think differently. It will make you think differently about yourself, about situations, about circumstances and about others. Faith will make you think in a way that is contrary to what would normally be thought. It will make you think you can, when odds

Chapter 14: Fear vs. Faith

tell you that you can't. Proverbs 23:7 says, *"As a man thinks in his heart, so is he."* Your thoughts form your future! The Bible says that we are transformed by the renewing of our minds. It says let this mind that is in Christ Jesus be in you. When you begin to think differently, you will see yourself, your world and all of those around you begin to look different. Say this out loud: I am loved, I am forgiven and I am accepted! Say, I am! I can! And I will! Sometimes you have to speak by faith that which you don't feel in theory. Faith will make you think differently than you normally would.

>**Fear Will Make You:**

5. Believe What You Wouldn't Normally Believe. Belief is a choice and what you believe will determine what you experience. Your mind will play tricks on you if you let it. Fear will make you believe things that in reality don't even exist or may never happen. It will create scenarios in your mind that may never come to fruition. Fear will exaggerate and exacerbate every thought or scenario. Fear will make you believe what you normally wouldn't believe.

>**Faith Will Make You:**

5. Believe What You Wouldn't Normally Believe. Faith is about believing before you see, not seeing before you believe. The Bible tells us that all things are possible to those who believe and faith makes that possible. Faith will make you believe what you normally wouldn't believe.

FEAR AND FAITH BOTH ENGAGE BELIEF

I believe we all have faith to some degree even if it is not Biblically based or Christ centered. You can put faith in many things. You can also put faith in the wrong things or the wrong people as well. However, if you want to put faith in what matters and have a faith that is anchored, I believe it must be Biblically based and Christ centered. For those who have believed and put their faith in Christ, the Bible actually tells us that we have been given a measure of faith. Now, even if you are not a person of faith, I believe that you still possess and exercise faith, or at least in the sense of having confidence or trust in something or someone. This can be as simple as putting your faith in the belief that your car will start in the morning or that the kitchen chair will hold you up while you eat your breakfast. Faith simply put is: confidence, belief and trust. And in reality, most of us, even people of faith deal with fear on some level or another, even if it's being afraid of what others may think about us.

However, most fears stem from occurrences that are beyond our control or from a lack of trust. Faith is trust. Fear threatens what brings confidence, belief and trust. Fear and faith are diametrically opposed. However, fear and faith both exist because of belief.

Chapter 14: Fear vs. Faith

Fear, for the most part, believes, assumes or anticipates something that is uncertain, unpleasant, dangerous or concerning. While, on the other hand, faith believes in something that is good, hopeful and trustworthy. Simply put, fear expects bad and faith expects good.

Fear will distort the good and exaggerate the bad. It will inhibit, impede and interfere. Fear will use the unknown to keep you from experiencing something better than you could ever know. Someone said, *"Everything that you have ever wanted is on the other side of fear."* Fear left unchallenged will keep you where you are. It will keep you bound. It will immobilize you. It is a deceptive foe that will steal your joy and rob you of your peace. Fear will challenge your faith and, left undealt with, fear could eventually undermine it. Fear will keep you from moving forward if you allow it to. But you can't allow it to; you must take a stand!

You must stand against its attempts to control you in a negative way. We all have fears, but pushing past your fear will determine what you experience. Winning the battle over unhealthy fear will establish peace in your life. Don't let fear dictate your decisions. Don't allow fear to determine what you do or don't do. Don't allow fear to determine the outcome of any scenario of your life. The more you learn to stand against fear, the more you will experience what you truly desire.

You can overcome fear by establishing a Biblical based Christ centered faith. Faith is about believing. It is about hoping. It's about having confidence and an assurance. So many entities, organizations and people use fear to control. They use fear to manipulate and gain access to vulnerabilities which in turn gives them more power and control over an individual. Even religion will use fear and intimidation. But, nonetheless, a Bible based Christ centered faith is not about religion, it's about a relationship with a person named Jesus Christ who came to liberate you and set you free! Being controlled by fear will keep things the way they are. But trusting in Christ creates possibilities for things to change for the better. Staying bound by fear will keep you from moving forward and from seeing things actually change or become different. A relationship with Christ and engagement in God's word will give you a foundation for things to be different.

The good news is when you put your faith in God and in His word it gives you a foundation that is unshakeable,

Chapter 14: Fear vs. Faith

even when you experience fear. The Bible is our faith feeder! Faith comes by hearing and hearing by the Word of God. The Bible is a book of hope. It is a book of restoration. It records and establishes your right and authority to be an overcomer. It points to righteousness over sin. Life over death! Light over darkness! Hope over hopelessness! And faith over fear! The Word is established by God and fulfilled through the person of Jesus Christ. Jesus came to empower us. It's recorded in God's Word Him saying over and over again: *"Do not be afraid!"*

Hebrews 11 says, *"Without Faith it is impossible to please God."* Faith is trusting God even when it doesn't make sense from your limited perspective. Faith and trust can give you victory over fear!

1. Faith is the beginning of all things.
2. Faith pleases God.
3. Faith allows you to receive salvation.
4. Faith gives you access to God.
5. Faith is required, to live the life God desires for you to live.
6. Faith empowers you with hope and establishes trust.
7. Faith gives you the power and authority to overcome fear.

I Was AFRAID of That!

Faith is the beginning of all things. However, having faith and relinquishing trust can be scary. That's because you don't know, see, or understand how things are going to turn out! And that can be scary. However, faith is not taking matters into your own hands; it's putting 'it' in God's hands and trusting Him for the best outcome. Remember, God knows what's best for you. Although you can't see the end result, God can. You can trust the 'unknown' to a God who knows what's unknown to you! And, He not only knows what's unknown to you, He knows you better than anyone else does. The reality is, if you're going to put your belief and trust in something, why not put it in faith, hope and love instead of fear, despair and hate?

Fear is an illusion that can distort reality and keep you from knowing, seeing, or experiencing what's on the other side of what you fear the most. Don't allow what you fear the most, to keep you from what you desire the most. Don't allow fear to determine what you do. Let faith determine what you do. Don't allow fear to dictate your decisions. Let faith dictate your decisions. Don't allow fear to keep you from a future you never realized you could have. Let faith unlock a future you didn't think was possible. Trust God and allow your fear to diminish while allowing your faith to be strengthened in Him.

Chapter 15

Antidotes to Fear

FACE IT OR FORFEIT FREEDOM

You have just read an entire chapter on fear versus faith. So let me start off by saying that faith undoubtedly is the greatest antidote to fear that there is. However, having faith doesn't mean that anything bad will never happen or that danger or fearful moments will never occur. But, your faith will help you to see difficulties as lessons and danger as an opportunity to use wisdom and to trust God for the best outcome. You must ask God for the grace and strength to see your setbacks, situations and scenarios from His vantage point. In exchange, this will help you find courage and establish strength for what you have to face. Fear doesn't automatically go away. It goes away when you believe that you are safe and that you are capable of handling whatever comes your way. By God's grace and through His strength and help, you can face anything. It's all about facing fear and counteracting the negative effects that it may have had on you. That's what an antidote does.

I Was AFRAID of That!

An antidote is something that counteracts the effects of something else. There are numerous and varying antidotes in regard to fear. Some of them are common sense, intelligence and sound judgement. But, you will also need courage, wisdom and strength to help you stand against fear. You will never conquer what you don't have the courage to face. Avoidance is not the answer when it comes to advancing over fear in your life. Remember, isolating yourself only reinforces fear. If you choose to continually stay safe rather than to face your fear, you will constantly avoid situations, experiences, activities and people. You will never learn to counteract the effects that fear is causing in your life by practicing avoidance. You must learn to face fear if you are going to live in freedom.

Fear will produce a result. It will affect situations. Fear will influence you to either do something or not to do something. An antidote will help counteract the effect of an emotion, action or a thought. An antidote will help counteract what fear has caused. Fear is *an unpleasant often strong emotion caused by anticipation or awareness of danger.* An antidote is *a remedy to counteract or correct the effects of something. It is the legal means to recover a right to something that was lost or to prevent a setback from something negative that*

Chapter 15: Antidotes to Fear

has been experienced. So, an antidote to fear would be anything that counteracts the effects of something that fear has caused. It could counteract any lack, grief, strife or loss that fear has made happen. An antidote would help bring a resolution to any situation that fear has hindered, held back or held up in your life. It would help bring about reconciliation for anything that could have produced profound progress or might have been constructive in making you stronger, better or more prosperous.

FEAR WHAT MATTERS

A *"result-producing"* antidote to fear would be fearing the right thing. What do I mean by that? What I mean is that so many times we fear the wrong things. We fear the things that may never happen. We fear those things that only exist in our minds and not in reality. We fear many things that really won't cause us harm or put us in a dangerous situation, but we allow that fear to stop us anyway. We fear the untimely, the unknown and the uncertain. But, what if we feared what mattered, or what if we feared what would make a difference or produce forward motion or positive progress in our lives? If you are going to be afraid, be afraid of never accomplishing your dreams. Be afraid of never trying something new. If you are going to be afraid, be afraid of things never being any different. Be afraid of missing out. Be afraid of never knowing love or finding freedom. If you are going to be afraid, be afraid of what matters, and don't be afraid of what doesn't matter. Put fear in its rightful place and begin to fear what matters the most! Stop fearing what can be lost and start anticipating what can be gained!

Instead of being afraid of going back to school, what if you were afraid not to. What if the equation of not going back to school produced a greater fear than going back to school? What if instead of being afraid of trying something new because you were afraid you were going to fail, you would be more afraid of not trying it at all because you realize that you could succeed? Be afraid of not walking in freedom more than you fear never being free. Be more afraid of not experiencing what you truly desire to experience, than you are afraid that things will never change or be different. The fear of the *"right thing"* should give you the courage to try again and the courage to do what needs to be done in order to experience what you truly desire. And, your new found courage should produce a decisive determination, that, in time, will grow your faith. Do what is right and do what will produce the result you desire. Do what you need to do in spite of

Chapter 15: Antidotes to Fear

what you fear and see what happens. One of the ways you can do this is by implementing an antidote. An antidote is the action initiative that will help you either stand against fear or counteract the negative effects that it has had on your life.

LET'S START HERE

There are so many antidotes to help you stand against fear or to counteract its negative effects, if I listed them all it could be an entire book. Therefore, I want to look at just a few that I feel are valuable and vital to your standing against fear and counteracting its negative effects.

Here are some antidotes to help you stand against fear and to counteract its negative effects. Included are the activities that will activate these antidotes in your life:

1. **<u>Pray</u>. Prayer is an antidote to fear.** (1) Prayer is communication with God. (2) Prayer is believing the promises of God's Word. (3) Prayer is seeking God, His will and His way of doing things. (4) Prayer is transferring what concerns you to a concerned God who cares for you and about you. (5) Prayer is bringing God, His peace and His presence into your situation and asking Him to help you. Prayer is talking to God and trusting Him with the outcome.

I Was **AFRAID** *of That!*

When you don't know what to pray, just say, "Jesus." When you don't know what to pray, pray: "Lord let your Kingdom come and your will be done in earth as it is in heaven!" There is no sorrow, sickness, pain, disappointment or suffering in heaven. There is also no fear! Lord, let your Kingdom come and your will be done! Amen.

Here's a prayer I used in a message that I did on trust. Pray it in faith and allow God's peace to surround you as you begin to trust Him in every area of your life:

"Lord give me the courage to step outside of what is safe and comfortable as I trust you to cover me with Your all sufficient grace. Holy Spirit teach me how to grow my capacity to handle life's challenges. May I have a posture of trust and an expectation of good. Thank you for your faithfulness to me. Even when I don't see it, You are my refuge and strength. You are a very present help in the time of trouble. I have no real reason to fear because Your love and Your grace surround me like a shield. So I receive Your peace now, knowing that love has been perfected. And I know and believe that perfect love casts out all fear. Your love surrounds me now and I thank you for it, In Jesus name. Amen"

Chapter 15: Antidotes to Fear

2. <u>**Be Courageous!**</u> **Courage is an antidote to fear.** Courage is not the absence of fear, but rather it is the power of the mind to overcome fear. It takes courage to face fear, but you will never conquer what you won't face. Faith without works is dead and faith without courage will produce minimal results. You can have all the faith in the world, but if you don't have the courage to act upon what you believe, you will never see the results that you desire to see! It takes action! Action is an antidote to fear. You have to act upon what you believe. David had faith in God when he faced the giant, Goliath, but he had to have courage when he released the stone to conquer that giant. If you are going to see the giant of fear fall in your life, you will have to have faith in God, but you will also have to have the courage to face what you fear.

3. <u>**Have Faith!**</u> **Faith is an antidote to fear.** Faith is given by God, but it has to be developed by you. Just like in the natural, what you feed grows, and what you don't doesn't; the same goes for faith. You have to feed your faith and starve your fears! That is, if you want to live in freedom and have peace. Not once in the Bible does it say, *"Grieve Not!"* or *"Sorrow Not!"* or *"Cry Not!"* It does,

however, say, "FEAR NOT!" So I take that as a commandment, not a suggestion. The only way to "fear not", is to have faith in the fact that there is hope in God through Christ Jesus who loves us. Hope is not wishful thinking; hope is a heightened expectation. Hope is an antidote to fear. It's an expectation of good, not bad and an expectation of hope, not hopelessness. You not only have to feed your faith and have hope, but you also have to focus on the right thing. What you focus on gets your attention and what gets your attention determines your direction. When Peter stepped out of the boat on faith and began to walk on the water toward Jesus, he didn't sink until he took his eyes off of Jesus. The waves and wind were a distraction that broke his focus and created fear. However, Jesus carried Peter right back through the wind and waves that caused him to fear in the first place. Have faith and fear not! Just like Jesus carried Peter back through wind and waves, He will be with you in every area of your life. No matter what you face or no matter what you fear, focus on Him! Put your faith in Him and fear not!

Conclusion

Displacing Fear at the Core of Your Life

FINDING A NEW FOUND FREEDOM

Fear has hindered me in so many areas of my life for way too long! I have had to battle and fight. And I have had to learn to face the unknown and the uncertain with a confidence and a courage that reminds me that God is for me and that He is more than enough! I have had to learn to take thoughts captive and I have had to intentionally decipher and discern what is the truth and what is reality. I have also had to come to terms with what is a figment of my own imagination or an exaggeration of my own self-doubt that is feeding my insecurity and causing me to fear or to be anxious. However, when I have faced what I have feared, I've usually realized there wasn't as much to fear as I thought there was to begin with. Fear is sometimes like a bully that just needs to be stood up to and proven wrong. God is with you and He is for you! And I am standing with you and I am believing for you! I am believing that any fear that has held you back or has hindered you in any way will be displaced with a new

found faith, strength and a courage that will empower you to overcome your fears.

I am believing that you will find freedom like I have. But, I also confess to you that I have allowed fear to hinder me in many ways, for way too long. Anyway, here are a few of the many fears that I have dealt with in my lifetime:

- The Fear of Being Wrong
- The Fear of Being Misunderstood
- The Fear of Being Rejected
- The Fear of Growing Old
- The Fear of Dying
- The Fear of the Unknown
- The Fear of Heights

Now when I look at my list, there is something that stands out to me: these fears have a common connection! There are fears in this list that are connected and that could be grouped together because of their similarity. There is a definite thread that these groups share in common. As I was typing this list of fears, I typed what first came to mind in regard to my greatest fears. But, after I had typed the list and looked at it again, I recognized how connected some of these fears actually were. These fears have a root that connects them and I want you to know that

Conclusion: Displacing Fear at the Core of Your Life

most fears do have a root that connects them. And when the root of the fear is revealed, the power that that particular fear has diminishes greatly. For example, the fear of being wrong, the fear of being misunderstood and the fear of being rejected are all connected. They are connected through the thread of the fear of failure, or failing in the sense of letting someone down or disappointing someone. The fear of failure can also make you feel as if you have failed someone or maybe disappointed someone by not communicating clearly. Nonetheless, they all have a root and that root is the "fear of failure." So, when the root of this fear is revealed you can stand against the emotion, perception or feeling that it is causing by declaring the truth. In this case, in regard to the "fear of failure", you can defeat this fear by realizing that "failure is not final" because "you serve a God of second chances."

The fear of growing old, the fear of dying, the fear of the unknown and the fear of heights all have a similar connection and root as well. The root that ties these fears together is the fear of things being beyond my control, or the fear of the unknown. When this root is revealed, you can stand against it by declaring the truth that there is nothing beyond God's ability and or knowledge. And remind yourself that you can trust the unknown to a God who knows and Who is proven and faithful. When things are beyond your control, they are not beyond God's ability. These are fears that I deal with and these are the roots and similarities of these fears. However, I believe that if you look at the fears that you deal with in your life, you will see the same similarities and/or roots that tie them together as well.

Most fears have a similarity or connection, and most fears have a common root. When these similarities that connect these fears and the roots that feed them are revealed, it is then easier to displace this fear at the core of your life. *I Was Afraid of That!* is all about helping you displace unhealthy fear at the core of your life. This book's purpose is to help you face those fears that hinder you and stifle you, endeavoring to stop you from being everything God intended you to be. I believe that there is always a root that causes fear to be established in your life. I also believe that when this root is revealed, you can be healed and empowered to rise above it. Then you can walk right past what you fear into a newfound freedom that will produce a greater peace, joy and contentment that will be greater than you have ever known in your life. I'm weary of seeing fear affect people in a negative way!

Conclusion: Displacing Fear at the Core of Your Life

I'm tired of seeing fear defeat you! That's why I wrote this book, to help enlighten you so that you may be empowered to rise above any fear that tries to hinder you or stop you, both now and in the future.

I believe that fear either knowingly or unknowingly hinders so many practical areas of our lives. I also believe that it is a silencer and inhibitor in a variety of ways. Fear will keep you from enjoying the simplest moments of life and it will endeavor to stop you from experiencing the most intimate moments of life as well. Fear is a thief! Fear is a liar! Fear is stifling and it will stop you from enjoying life if you allow it to do so. It will cause you to freeze when you should flee and it will cause you to be silent when you should speak up. Fear will cause you to doubt when you should believe and it will cause you to feel hopeless when you should be hopeful. Where there is fear there is no peace. Where there is fear there is no hope. Where there is fear there is no freedom. Where there is fear, there is no joy.

I want to see you have joy and peace and hope! I want you to be empowered to speak up when you need to! I want to see you believe instead of doubt! I want to see you be free and enjoy life! I want to see you displace

any unhealthy fear that is at the core of your life. Too many decisions, ideas, dreams, ventures, investments, and opportunities have been left unaccomplished or not even begun at all, because people were afraid of something. Nonetheless, I don't believe that there will ever be a time that when you are faced with something new, untimely, uncertain or unknown that fear won't present itself. That's why I wrote this book. I want to see unhealthy fear that lies at the core of your life be displaced and replaced by confidence, courage and a calmness to face fear head on. I want to see you live your dreams and experience your best life now! I want for you to be able to say with confidence and assurance, *"I Was Afraid of That!"* That's right, past tense.

A FEW MORE THOUGHTS AND A PRAYER

I pray that you have been enlightened, empowered, strengthened and set free as you have read this book. It is my hope that you are able to face your fears with a new found confidence. I am also believing that this book has helped equip you, empower you and that it has enable you to face your fears and ultimately defeat them. I expectantly assured that you are more capable now than you have ever been to say, *"I Was Afraid of That!"*: That's right, past tense.

Conclusion: Displacing Fear at the Core of Your Life

Here are twelve ways that you can continue to displace unhealthy fear at the core of your life:

1. Accept Christ as Your Personal Savior, if You Haven't Already.
2. Pray.
3. Attend a Bible Believing Church.
4. Read the Word.
5. Develop a Lifestyle of Worship.
6. Renew Your Mind.
7. Adjust Your Focus.
8. Plead the Blood of Christ Over: Your Life, Your Spouse, Your Children, Your Health, Your Home, Your Finances, Your Family and Your Friends.
9. Trust God to Do What You Can't Do.
10. Surround Yourself with Helpful, Healthy People.
11. Pray for the Courage to Face What Needs to Be Confronted.
12. Build Your Faith and Face Your Fears.

Pray This Prayer:

Lord, I believe that You are with me. I believe that you will never leave me, nor forsake me. I thank you even now that Your perfect love casts out all fear. I ask for You to reveal the root of any fear in my life that is hindering me and I ask You to take those fears from me now and replace them with your love and peace. Thank you Lord that I can now say, "I Was Afraid of That!": That's right, past tense. In Jesus name, Amen!

So do not fear, for I am with you; do not be dismayed, for I am your God. I will strengthen you and help you; I will uphold you with my righteous right hand. - Isaiah 41:10

Special Thanks

I would like to thank Becky Watson for her help in making this book easier for you to read by making sentences and thoughts make sense and become clearer. And I thank her for catching all of those misspelled words and incomplete sentences in such a timely manner! She was the first one to read it and she is greatly appreciated for doing so!

I would like to thank Jeremy Knotts who created an external hard drive for me to continue writing this book when my computer crashed and for letting me use his computer to do graphic work for my book and to update my website. This book wouldn't have been completed without your help and generosity.

I would like to thank Heath Honaker for being such a good friend and for setting the format of this book in regards to headers, chapters and page numbers. Also a huge shout out for recreating this book cover when my computer crashed. You definitely saved the day! And for Heath and his wife Bev for going the extra mile in regard to the final edits and finishing touches.

For More Resources go to: www.robcollins.org

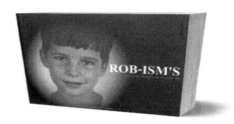

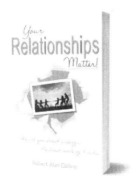

Follow Rob on Social Media:

About the Author

Rob Collins is a husband, father, pastor, and author. He is passionate about people and believes in hope for every person through Jesus Christ. It's Rob's desire **to** equip people to be empowered with: passion, purpose, and perseverance. His messages will inspire you to believe for more, and challenge you to reach your full potential in Christ. His words of passion are from the heart, and they will speak to you wherever you are in your journey of life and faith. It is his desire that through a growing relationship with Jesus Christ you will find hope and peace. Rob also believes the Word is the foundation of faith in which you can find your compass for direction, and your purpose for life.

Rob has been ministering for over 37 years. Through the years he has spoken at churches, conferences, colleges, and on radio and television. He travels and speaks at various venues for a variety of occasions. Rob has written articles in several publications and he is also the author of: *"Robism's"*, *When They Close the Lid*, *Your Relationships Matter* and *I Was Afraid of That!* Rob has a deep love for his family. He resides in Ohio with his wife Kelly, his two daughters Megan Brooke and Madison Grace, and their dog, Toby Mac.

[1] https://www.biblestudytools.com/dictionary/fear/
[ii] https://www.verywellmind.com/the-psychology-of-fear-2671696
[iii] https://www.verywellmind.com/the-psychology-of-fear-2671696
[iv] Kozlowska K, Walker P, McLean L, Carrive P. Fear and the defense cascade: Clinical implications and management. Harv Rev Psychiatry. 2015;23(4):263-287. doi:10.1097/HRP.0000000000000065
[v] https://www.verywellmind.com/the-psychology-of-fear-2671696
[vi] https://www.verywellmind.com/the-psychology-of-fear-2671696
[vii] https://thesalesblog.com/2019/05/31/facing-the-two-types-of-fears/
[viii] https://thesalesblog.com/2019/05/31/facing-the-two-types-of-fears/
[ix] https://thesalesblog.com/2019/05/31/facing-the-two-types-of-fears/
[x] Alfred Lord Tennyson
[xi] Robert Sharma
[xii] Luke 6:38
[xiii] Philippians 4:19
[xiv] Psalm 37:5
[xv] Dr. Henry Cloud Instagram meme